# SHEPHERD'S NOTES

# Shepherd's Notes Titles Available

## SHEPHERD'S NOTES COMMENTARY SERIES

### Old Testament

9-780-805-490-282 Genesis
9-780-805-490-565 Exodus
9-780-805-490-695 Leviticus, Numbers
9-780-805-490-275 Deuteronomy
9-780-805-490-589 Joshua, Judges
9-780-805-490-572 Ruth, Esther
9-780-805-490-633 1 & 2 Samuel
9-780-805-490-077 1 & 2 Kings
9-780-805-490-649 1 & 2 Chronicles
9-780-805-491-944 Ezra, Nehemiah
9-780-805-490-060 Job
9-780-805-493-399 Psalms 1-50

9-780-805-493-405 Psalms 51-100
9-780-805-493-412 Psalms 101-150
9-780-805-490-169 Proverbs
9-780-805-490-596 Ecclesiastes, Song of
                   Solomon
9-780-805-491-975 Isaiah
9-780-805-490-701 Jeremiah, Lamentations
9-780-805-490-787 Ezekiel
9-780-805-490-152 Daniel
9-780-805-493-269 Hosea, Obadiah
9-780-805-493-344 Jonah, Zephaniah
9-780-805-490-657 Haggai, Malachi

### New Testament

9-781-558-196-889 Matthew
9-780-805-490-718 Mark
9-780-805-490-046 Luke
9-781-558-196-933 John
9-781-558-196-919 Acts
9-780-805-490-053 Romans
9-780-805-493-252 1 Corinthians
9-780-805-493-351 2 Corinthians
9-781-558-196-902 Galatians
9-780-805-493-276 Ephesians

9-781-558-196-896 Philippians, Colossians,
                   Philemon
9-780-805-490-008 1 & 2 Thessalonians
9-781-558-196-926 1 & 2 Timothy, Titus
9-780-805-493-368 Hebrews
9-780-805-490-183 James
9-780-805-490-190 1 & 2 Peter & Jude
9-780-805-492-149 1, 2 & 3 John
9-780-805-490-176 Revelation

## SHEPHERD'S NOTES CHRISTIAN CLASSICS

9-780-805-493-474 *Mere Christianity,*
                   C. S. Lewis
9-780-805-493-535 *The Problem of Pain/*
                   *A Grief Observed,*
                   C. S. Lewis
9-780-805-491-999 *The Confessions,*
                   Augustine
9-780-805-492-002 *Calvin's Institutes*
9-780-805-493-948 *Miracles,* C. S. Lewis

9-780-805-491-968 *Lectures to My Students,*
                   Charles Haddon
                   Spurgeon
9-780-805-492-200 *The Writings of Justin*
                   *Martyr*
9-780-805-493-450 *The City of God,*
                   Augustine
9-780-805-491-982 *The Cost of Discipleship,*
                   Bonhoeffer

## SHEPHERD'S NOTES — BIBLE SUMMARY SERIES

9-780-805-493-771 Old Testament
9-780-805-493-788 New Testament

9-780-805-493-849 Life & Teachings of Jesus
9-780-805-493-856 Life & Letters of Paul

# SHEPHERD'S NOTES

*When you need a guide through the Scriptures*

# *Matthew*

HOLMAN
REFERENCE

NASHVILLE, TENNESSEE

978-1-5581-9688-9

Dewey Decimal Classification: 226.2
Subject Heading: BIBLE. N.T. MATTHEW
Library of Congress Card Catalog Number: 97–25012

**Library of Congress Cataloging-in-Publication Data**

Matthew / Dana Gould, editor
  p.  cm.—(Shepherd's notes)
  Includes bibliographical references.
  ISBN 1–55819–688–9 (tp)
        1. Bible. N.T. Matthew—Study and teaching.
  I. Gould, Dana, 1951–.   II. Series.
BS2576.M37 1997
226.2'0071—DC21

97–25012
CIP

17 18 19 20 21        16 15 14 13 12

# CONTENTS

# FOREWORD

Dear Reader:

*Shepherd's Notes* are designed to give you a quick, step-by-step overview of every book of the Bible. They are not meant to be a substitute for the biblical text; rather, they are study guides intended to help you explore the wisdom of Scripture in personal or group study and to apply that wisdom successfully in your own life.

*Shepherd's Notes* guide you through both the main themes of each book of the Bible and illuminate fascinating details through appropriate commentary and reference notes. Historical and cultural background information brings the Bible into sharper focus.

Six different icons, used throughout the series, call your attention to historical-cultural information, Old Testament and New Testament references, word pictures, unit summaries, and personal application for everyday life.

Whether you are a novice or a veteran at Bible study, I believe you will find *Shepherd's Notes* a resource that will take you to a new level in your mining and applying the riches of Scripture.

In Him,

David R. Shepherd
Editor-in-Chief

## DESIGNED FOR THE BUSY USER

*Shepherd's Notes* for Matthew is designed to provide an easy-to-use tool for getting a quick handle on the book's key features and for gaining an understanding of Matthew's Gospel. Information available in more difficult-to-use reference works has been incorporated into the Shepherd's Notes format. This brings you the benefits of many more advanced and expensive works packed into one small volume.

*Shepherd's Notes* are for laymen, pastors, teachers, small-group leaders, and participants, as well as the classroom student. Enrich your personal study or quiet time. Shorten your class or small-group preparation time as you gain valuable insights into the truths of God's Word that you can pass along to your students or group members.

## DESIGNED FOR QUICK ACCESS

Those with time constraints will especially appreciate the timesaving features built into Shepherd's Notes. All features are intended to aid a quick and concise encounter with the heart of the message.

*Concise Commentary.* Matthew's narrative is replete with characters, places, and events. Short sections provide quick "snapshots" of the running narrative, highlighting important points.

*Outlined Text.* A comprehensive outline covers the entire text of Matthew. This is a valuable feature for following the narrative's flow, and it allows for a quick, easy way to locate a particular passage.

*Shepherd's Notes.* These summary statements appear at the close of every key section of the narrative. While functioning in part as a quick summary, they also deliver the essence of the message presented in the sections they cover.

*Icons*. Various icons in the margin highlight recurring themes in Matthew and aid in selective searching or tracing of those themes.

*Sidebars and Charts*. These specially selected features provide additional background information to your study or preparation. These include definitions as well as cultural, historical, and biblical information.

*Questions to Guide Your Study*. These thought-provoking questions and discussion starters are designed to encourage interaction with the truth and principles of God's Word.

## DESIGNED TO WORK FOR YOU

*Personal study*. Using the Shepherd's Notes with a passage of Scripture can enlighten your study and take it to a new level. At your fingertips is information that would require searching several volumes to find. In addition, many points of application occur throughout the volume, contributing to personal growth.

*Teaching*. Outlines frame the text of Matthew's narrative and provide a logical presentation of the message. Capsule thoughts designated as "Shepherd's Notes" provide summary statements for presenting the essence of key points and events. Application icons point out personal application of the message of Matthew's Gospel, and Historical Context and Cultural Context icons indicate where background information is supplied.

*Group Study*. Shepherd's Notes can be an excellent companion volume to use for gaining a quick but accurate understanding of the message of a Bible book. Each group member can benefit by having his or her own copy. The *Note's* format accommodates the study or the tracing of themes throughout Matthew. Leaders may use its flexible features to prepare for group sessions, or use them during group sessions. The guiding questions can spark discussion of the key points and truths of Matthew's message.

## LIST OF ICONS USED IN MATTHEW

 *Shepherd's Notes.* Placed at the end of each section, a capsule statement that provides the reader with the essence of the message of that section.

 *Old Testament Reference.* Used when the writer refers to Old Testament Scripture passages that are related or have a bearing on the passage's understanding or interpretation.

 *New Testament Reference.* Used when the writer refers to New Testament passages that are related to or have a bearing on the passage's understanding or interpretation.

 *Historical Background.* To indicate historical, cultural, geographical, or biographical information that sheds light on the understanding or interpretation of a passage.

 *Personal Application.* Used when the text provides a personal or universal application of truth.

 *Word Picture.* Indicates that the meaning of a specific word or phrase is illustrated so as to shed light on it.

The Gospel of Matthew has likely influenced more people than any other Christian book. Its role of influence probably began with its acceptance by Antioch, a great early Christian center. The greater use of Matthew comes in part from its first-place position in the New Testament. Also, only Matthew contains the Sermon on the Mount.

## AUTHOR

Early in the first century A.D., a Christian writer wrote this account of Jesus' life and teachings. This Gospel, like all four canonical Gospels, is anonymous. Nowhere in the Gospel does it actually disclose its author. Early tradition, however, attributed the work to Matthew, one of Jesus' twelve apostles.

## AUDIENCE

Early Church tradition meshes with the style and contents of the Gospel to suggest that Matthew wrote to a Jewish-Christian audience. It is difficult to narrow down the destination any further. A few ancient sources favored Palestine, perhaps Jerusalem. Modern scholars often propose Syria, particularly Antioch.

## PURPOSE

Matthew most likely wrote his Gospel for several reasons. (1) He wanted to convince non-Christian Jews of the truth of Christianity. (2) He sought to explain to Christians how their religion is the fulfillment of God's promises and patterns of activity in the Old Testament. (3) He wanted to give young believers basic instruction in Christian living. (4) He wanted to encourage his church in the midst of persecution from hostile authorities in both Jewish and Roman circles. (5) He desired to deepen Christian faith by supplying more details about Jesus' words and works.

## DATE AND PLACE OF WRITING

Hostility between the Jews and Jesus' followers on the pages of the Gospel has suggested to many that Matthew's Jewish-Christian church had decisively broken from the (non-Christian) synagogue. This often leads to dating of the Gospel to the mid-80s or later, after the synagogues allegedly introduced a curse on heretics (including Christians) into their liturgy of prayers. Quotations from the Apostolic Fathers suggests an upper limit for the dating around A.D. 100. As a result, most Bible scholars believe Matthew's Gospel was written about A.D. 80 to 90.

## DISTINCTIVES IN MATTHEW'S GOSPEL

Several distinctive characteristics are evident in Matthew.

- Because of its position, it is the most widely read book in the New Testament and has exerted the greatest influence on the world.
- Ten parables appear in Matthew that are not found in the other Gospels: the wheat and the weeds, the hidden treasure, the dragnet, the pearl of great price, the unmerciful servant, the laborers in the vineyard, the two sons, the wedding feast of the king's son, the ten maidens, and the talents.
- The only two parables recorded involving money are found in Matthew's Gospel: the unmerciful servant, the laborers in the vineyard.
- Of the four Gospels, only Matthew's makes specific mention of the Church.
- Matthew stressed "last things," the coming of the end time.

### HEADING (1:1)

This heading introduces the main character of Matthew's Gospel and describes His identity in terms of His Jewish heritage. The titles "Christ," "Son of David," and "Son of Abraham" held high significance for Matthew's audience.

### RECORD OF JESUS' ANCESTRY (1:2–17)

#### *Purpose of Matthew's Record*

Many people skip over the genealogies of the Bible. After all, lists of obscure, long-dead people are not very interesting. But Matthew had a definite purpose in starting his Gospel with Jesus' genealogy. The *linear genealogy,* which Matthew uses, seeks to show that the final person listed has a legitimate right to the position of honor the person occupies. Matthew wanted to establish Jesus as a legitimate descendant of David and rightful candidate for the messianic throne.

#### *Structure of the Record*

He divides the genealogy into three general sections (of fourteen entries), each covering a phase of Jewish history. The first section spans Abraham to David, the greatest king of Israel (vv. 2–6). The second section covers Jewish history from the time of David's son Solomon to the Babylonian exile (vv. 7–11). The third section includes the time up until the coming of Jesus, the Savior of all people (vv. 12–18).

#### *Special Features of the Record*

Matthew's genealogy contains several points of special interest.

*Mention of Four Women.* Contrary to Jewish tradition, Matthew includes four women in his

Matthew's Titles for Jesus

*Christ.* This is the Greek transliteration of the Hebrew term *Messiah,* which means "the anointed one."

*Son of David.* Points to the Messiah's link to Israel's most honored king and the fact that He is to be of royal blood.

*Son of Abraham.* Traces Jesus' lineage back to the founding father of the nation of Israel.

The inclusion of these four women shows (1) that God can use all kinds of people, even those who are conspicuously imperfect, in the carrying out of His plan and (2) that we see the solidarity of Jesus with sinful humanity. Jesus came to sinful human beings in order to break down barriers between God and human beings, Jew and Gentile, male and female, and the righteous and the unrighteous.

**Virgin Birth**

The virgin birth of Jesus is a fulfillment of Old Testament prophecy. Isaiah 7:14 tells us: "Therefore the Lord himself will give you a sign: The virgin will be with child and will give birth to a son, and will call him 'Immanuel.'"

Magi were wise men, priests, and astrologers who were students of the heavens and interpreters of dreams. Joseph and Mary received a visit from Magi whose interpretation of the stars led them to Palestine to find and honor the newborn King. They may have come from Babylon, Persia, or the Arabian desert.

genealogy. Moreover, these were not women one might expect to be included. Tamar was an adulteress (v. 3). Ruth, a Moabitess, was not a Jew (v. 5). Rahab was a harlot (v. 5), and Bathsheba, the wife of Uriah, had been wrongfully taken by David (v. 6). The factor that clearly applies to all four is that suspicions of illegitimacy surrounded their sexual activity and childbearing.

This suspicion fits perfectly with the circumstances that surrounded Mary, so Matthew immediately takes pains to refute it. In fact, the grammar of verse 16 makes clear that Joseph was not the human father of Jesus. The pronoun *whom* is feminine and therefore can refer only to Mary as the human parent of the Christ child.

*Joseph as Jesus' Legal Father.* Matthew, true to Jewish custom, traces Jesus' descent through Joseph, even though Joseph was not Jesus' real father. According to Jewish Law, however, Joseph, as Mary's husband, was Jesus' *legal* father.

## THE BIRTH OF JESUS THE MESSIAH (1:18–25)

Matthew begins his Gospel by recounting selected events surrounding Jesus' birth (about 4–6 B.C.). The rest of Matthew's "infancy narrative" is comprised of five quotations from the Old Testament and the stories that illustrate five ways those texts were fulfilled in Jesus (1:18–2:23). The first of these fulfillments is the virginal conception of Jesus. Matthew's account of Jesus' birth is written from Joseph's viewpoint. In contrast, Luke's Gospel narrates the event from Mary's point of view.

- *Matthew sees in the coming of Jesus the com-*
- *plete fulfillment of Isa. 7:14. That prophecy*
- *calls the son who would be born "Immanuel,"*
- *meaning "God with us."*

The Gifts of the Wise Men

Gold—the symbol of kingship.

Frankincense—associated with holiness and worship.

Myrrh—used in embalming the dead.

## QUESTIONS TO GUIDE YOUR STUDY

1. What is the value of Matthew's genealogical record to us?
2. What do the record's special features reveal?
3. How do Old Testament prophecies support Jesus' birth as that of the Messiah?

# MATTHEW 2

Matthew opens this chapter by providing the time and place of Jesus' birth, which took place approximately five miles south of Jerusalem, at the time when Herod was king.

The Magi

Verses 4–6 contain the second of Matthew's five fulfillment quotations of prophecy: "But you, Bethlehem Ephrathah, though you are small among the clans of Judah, out of you will come for me one who will be ruler over Israel, whose origins are from of old, from ancient times" (Mic. 5:2).

## VISIT FROM THE WISE MEN (2:1–12)

A group of wise men, or Magi, journeyed from the East to pay homage to the newborn Jewish king. We don't know how many were in the group. The traditional idea that there were three stems from the mention of three kinds of gifts.

This unusual event occurred close to the time of Jesus' birth, but its exact time is unknown. These men studied the heavens and had seen a new star which they interpreted as heralding the birth of the long-hoped-for Messiah of the Jews.

When Herod learned that the wise men were searching for the Jewish king, he became deeply

**Dreams in the Bible**

In the Ancient Near Eastern world, dreams had great significance. In some cases, they provided information about the future and were used to show the dreamer the right decision to make. The dreams of common people were important to them, but the dreams of kings and holy men or women were important on a national or international scale. As Matthew's narrative shows, God used dreams as a vehicle of revelation in the birth and early days of Jesus.

From the fact that Jesus' family stayed in Egypt until Herod died, Matthew sees fulfillment of the words of the prophet Hosea: "When Israel was a child, I loved him, and out of Egypt I called my son" (11:1). Matthew looks deeper and sees Jesus repeating the experience of the Israelites by being called out of Egypt.

troubled. He was jealous of any threat to his throne. Herod implemented a plan to murder all male infants in an effort to make sure he had killed the new Jewish king. In a dream, God warned the wise men not to go back to Herod. They obeyed God's warning and returned by another route to their home country.

■ *This event shows God's intention to bless*
■ *Gentiles as well as Jews through His Son.*
■ *The openness and obedience of these Gentiles*
■ *stand in sharp contrast to the hostility*
■ *toward Jesus on the part of Herod.*

## JOSEPH AND MARY'S ESCAPE FROM KING HEROD (2:13–18)

Herod did not take lightly the failure of the Magi to return to him. His order to kill all the male children two years of age or under put Jesus in danger.

But God intervened. In a dream, He warned Joseph to leave Bethlehem quickly, taking Jesus and Mary with him. Joseph obeyed at once, and they fled to Egypt, a Roman province not under Herod's rule. There they found safe haven from Herod and his murderous schemes. Joseph and his family remained in Egypt until Herod's death.

■ *Although Bethlehem had become a place of*
■ *death and sorrow, Jesus' birth signals the*
■ *promise of future restoration and life.*

## JOSEPH AND MARY'S RETURN TO NAZARETH (2:19–23)

After Herod the Great died, and the danger to Jesus was past, God once again sent an angel to give instructions to Joseph in a dream. Joseph, Mary, and Jesus were to return to Israel. As before, Joseph obeyed without questioning.

 Matthew sees Jesus' residence in Nazareth as a fulfillment of the prophets' words that the Messiah would be known as a Nazarene. Matthew's statement is somewhat difficult to interpret, because no mention of Nazareth can be found in the Old Testament. One explanation, however, may shed some light on Matthew's possible meaning. Isaiah had prophesied that people would despise the Servant of the Lord. Some of the contempt shown for Jesus can be seen in the words of Nathanael who, when told about Jesus, asked, "Can anything good come from there?" (John 1:46).

■ *Jesus' residence in the despised city Naza-*
■ *reth, following His birth in a humble village,*
■ *speaks greatly of His humility. This was,*
■ *however, completely in line with His charac-*
■ *ter as revealed in Phil. 2:5–13.*

## QUESTIONS TO GUIDE YOUR STUDY

1. Note how God used the Old Testament Scriptures to convince Joseph and Herod. Does God still use Scripture to convince His people?
2. What events of Matthew 2 point to Jesus as the Messiah?

Nazareth. This place name means "branch." It was located in the hill country of lower Galilee about halfway between the Sea of Galilee and the Mediterranean Sea. It was a small village in Jesus' day and did not enjoy prominence until its association with Jesus. To some, Nazareth was a despised city (cf. John 1:46).

The "Hidden Years"

Matthew remains silent about the thirty or so years after Jesus' family settled in Nazareth. Apart from the one episode of Jesus teaching in the temple at the age of twelve (Luke 2:41–52), none of the four canonical Gospels describes anything about His intervening years. In striking contrast, the apocryphal gospels fill Jesus' "hidden years" with all kinds of miraculous exploits, esoteric teaching, and exotic travels.

**Early Homes of Jesus**

*Bethlehem.* This place name means "house of bread." It was a humble, unassuming village located only five miles from Jerusalem. A field southeast of the town has been identified as the place where the angel of the Lord appeared to shepherds in the middle of the night.

*Egypt.* Egypt was a land in the northeast corner of Africa, separated from Palestine by the Sinai wilderness. Home to one of the earliest civilizations, it had an important cultural and political influence on Israel. Egypt afforded a natural haven for first-century Jews. A large Jewish community had lived there for several centuries, and even from Old Testament times, Egypt had often provided a refuge when danger threatened Israel (e.g., 1 Kings 11:40; 2 Kings 25:26; Zech. 10:10) .

"In the desert prepare the way for the Lord; make straight in the wilderness a highway for our God" (Isa. 40:3).

3. What part did dreams play in the birth and infancy of Jesus?

# MATTHEW 3

In this chapter Matthew jumps abruptly from the events surrounding Jesus' birth to the time of His adult life. He begins this section with the sudden appearance of John the Baptist in the Judean wilderness.

## THE MISSION OF JOHN THE BAPTIST (3:1–6)

### His Preaching

John's preaching called for the people to repent as he announced the nearness of the "kingdom of heaven" (v. 2). That phrase has the same meaning as the "kingdom of God" and refers to God's kingly rule.

The most important component of John's message concerned his relationship to the Messiah. John preached a coming judgment that the Messiah would carry out. The unusual fact about John's preaching and baptism was that he called Jews to baptism and repentance. In contrast, the Jews believed it was the Gentiles who needed to repent and be baptized.

### His Purpose

The people considered John's appearance as the fulfillment of Isaiah's prophecy: The passage in Isaiah speaks of God's coming to lead His people out of their exile in Babylon. It mentions a voice that cried out for a way to be made for the coming of the Lord. Matthew sees John the Baptist as that voice preparing the hearts of the people for the coming of the Messiah, who would lead them out of sin's exile.

*John's ministry accomplished three purposes:*

1. He prepared for the Messiah's coming by raising expectations and calling for repentance (v. 2).

2. He explained the nature of the Messiah's mission (v. 11; Luke 3:16).

3. He inaugurated the Messiah's ministry by baptizing Him (vv. 13–17; Mark 1:9–11; Luke 3:21–23).

■ *God sent John the Baptist as a voice to pre-*
■ *pare the hearts of the people for the coming*
■ *of the Messiah. John clearly taught that one's*
■ *faith is a matter of personal commitment, not*
■ *a reliance on ancestral pedigree.*

## JOHN'S CONFRONTATION WITH THE PHARISEES AND SADDUCEES (3:7–12)

Two groups of Jewish leaders appeared on the scene in Matthew's narrative: the Pharisees and Sadducees. These parties represented two of the main religious sects of Jesus' day. Most of the Jewish supreme court, the Sanhedrin, belonged to one of these two groups.

### John's View of the Jewish Leaders (vv. 7–10)

Members of both groups came to John for baptism, either out of curiosity or for public show. John compared them to snakes fleeing a grass fire, calling them a "brood of vipers!" The term *vipers* is in reference to their shrewdness and to the danger they posed to others. John's reaction indicates that he doubted their genuineness and did not heartily welcome them as prospective converts.

*Repentance* is one of the mistranslated, and often misunderstood, words of the Bible. The language of the New Testament has a word for *repent* and a different word for *sorry*. The tragedy of it is that we do not have an English word that reproduces exactly the meaning of the Greek word *metanoeo*, "to repent." Too often readers take the word *repent* to mean "to be sorry again." John did not call on the people to be sorry, but to change their ways. The word Matthew uses here is a change of mind or attitude that issues in a change of action. A person who truly repents turns from sin and submits his or her life to God's rule.

9

## Jewish Groups in Jesus' Day

| GROUP | MEANING OF THE NAME | BELIEFS | ACTIVITIES |
|---|---|---|---|
| Pharisees | "The separated ones" | Viewed entire O.T. as their authority; accepted oral law | Established and controlled synagogues |
| Sadducees | "The righteous ones" | Viewed only the Torah (Law) as their authority; opposed oral law | In charge of the temple and its services |
| Essenes | Unknown origin | Considered other literature as authoritative; held to very strict ascetics | Copied and studied manuscripts of the Law |
| Zealots | Refers to their religious zeal | Similar to Pharisees, but believed that God had right to rule over the Jews | Extremely opposed to Roman rule over Palestine |
| Herodians | Based on their support of the Herodian rulers | A political group, comprised of representatives of varied theological perspectives | Supported Herod and the Herodian dynasty |

### John's Baptism (vv. 11–12)

John described his baptism as one for "repentance" (v. 11). He looked ahead to the One who would appear after him who would baptize "with the Holy Spirit and with fire."

■ *Christians in every age must heed the same*
■ *warning John gave to the Pharisees and Sad-*

- ducees. *It isn't enough to trust in one's mem-*
- *berships or associations. Without the*
- *evidence of a changed life and perseverance*
- *of faith, all such grounds of trust prove futile.*

### THE BAPTISM OF JESUS (3:13–17)

Because baptism implies that a person has repented, John balked at baptizing Jesus. Jesus nevertheless requested baptism for a different reason. That reason was "to fulfill all righteousness." That is, His baptism would be doing God's will. John baptized Jesus by immersing Him in the water. His rising up from the water provided a picture of His death, burial, and resurrection.

- *The baptism of Jesus marked His entrance*
- *into public ministry and confirmed Him as*
- *the Son of God. The Holy Spirit came to*
- *anoint and empower Him for the mission that*
- *lay ahead.*

### QUESTIONS TO GUIDE YOUR STUDY

1. Describe John the Baptist's mission. What did he accomplish?
2. What does it mean to repent?
3. Why was it so important that Jesus be baptized?

**John the Baptist**

John the Baptist was a prophet from a priestly family. He preached a message of repentance, announced the coming of the Messiah, baptized Jesus, and was beheaded by Herod Antipas. John's clothing reminded the people of the ancient prophet Elijah (cf. 2 Kings 1:8). It was generally believed that Elijah would return just before the Messiah made His appearance. John wore camel's hair clothing with a leather girdle. His diet would be considered repulsive to most Westerners. He lived off the land, eating insects (such as locusts, an excellent source of protein) and wild honey (Matt. 3:4).

## MATTHEW 4

### JESUS' TEMPTATIONS IN THE WILDERNESS (4:1–11)

Immediately after Jesus' baptism, the Holy Spirit orchestrated the circumstances that permitted

**Temptation**

The word *tempt*, as used here, means "to solicit to sin." Both the Old and New Testaments make clear that God does not entice persons to sin, but both testaments indicate that God allows human beings to be tempted. The Bible refers to the temptation as coming from the "tempter," "devil," or "Satan." James 1:14 also tells us that "temptation comes from the lure of our own evil desires" (NLT). Persons are thus tempted by the tempter or from within themselves.

**The Devil**

The word *devil* in Greek, the language of the New Testament, means "accuser," as does the Hebrew word translated "Satan" in the Old Testament. Scripture teaches that Satan was a created being, an archangel, and the leader of the rebellious angels who became forever opposed to God and whose ultimate doom Christ's death ensured (e.g., Job 1–2; Zech. 3:1–2; 1 Chron. 21:1; Luke 10:18; Rev. 20).

the devil to test Jesus' understanding of His sonship. The Spirit led Jesus into the wilderness, where He fasted forty days and forty nights before the temptations took place.

### The First Temptation: To Win the World with Bread (vv. 2–4)

This temptation was twofold. One, Jesus had just spent forty days fasting in the wilderness, and He must have been very hungry! Second, the devil used that hunger to suggest a way for Jesus to use His powers.

### The Second Temptation: To Win the World with Amazing Feats (vv. 5–7)

Having failed with the first temptation, the devil tried again. He took Jesus to the highest portion of the temple and told Jesus to throw Himself off. The devil quoted Psalm 91:11–12 to Jesus, which promised God's protection for those who put their trust in Him. But Jesus realized that deliberately placing oneself in danger to force God's protection would be presumptuous.

### The Third Temptation: To Win the World with Satan's Methods (vv. 8–10)

The devil tried yet a third time. He showed Jesus "all the kingdoms of the world." He proposed to give Jesus all this if He would only bow down and worship Satan. Here Satan was implying that the good result (dominion over the world) would justify the evil means used to attain it.

The devil left defeated, his attempts to sway Jesus having failed. He would, however, try to tempt Jesus many times during His forthcoming ministry.

■ *Adam, the first man, gave in to Satan's testing, wanting to be like God Himself. But*

- *Jesus, who was God's Son, chose the way of*
- *service to His Father, wherever that way*
- *might lead.*

## JESUS' MINISTRY IN GALILEE (4:12–16)

 Jesus settled in a new town, Capernaum, which became the headquarters for His Galilean ministry. It was larger and more significant than Nazareth, and it was strategic because of its lakeside setting on the northwest shore of the Sea of Galilee. With this event, Matthew sees the fulfillment of Isa. 9:1–2. Here Jesus began preaching.

Verse 12 alludes to the fate of John the Baptist, which will be discussed in more detail in chapter 11.

- *Jesus begins His earthly ministry. In Him the*
- *kingdom of God was no longer future, but*
- *had now become present tense.*

## THE BEGINNING OF JESUS' MINISTRY (4:17–22)

### A Summary Statement of Jesus' Preaching (v. 17)

Matthew introduces Jesus' public ministry with a statement of the message of His preaching and teaching: "Repent, for the kingdom of heaven is near."

### Jesus Calls His First Disciples (vv. 18–22)

Jesus chose a close group of followers who could share in His work. So, early on He called four men to be His disciples. The first two, fishermen, were brothers named Andrew and Simon

God has promised believers the power to overcome temptation. First Corinthians 10:13 promises, "Remember that the temptations that come into your life are no different from what others experience. And God is faithful. He will keep the temptation from becoming so strong that you can't stand up against it. When you are tempted, he will show you a way out so that you will not give in to it" (NLT).

The English word *gospel* is from the New Testament Greek word *euangelion,* which means "good news." Prior to the second century, it always referred to oral communication.

Peter. We know from John's Gospel that Jesus was already acquainted with these two during the ministry of John the Baptist (John 1:40–42). Two other brothers, James and John, received Jesus' call. They, too, were fishermen and may also have known Jesus earlier.

## JESUS' TEACHING, PREACHING, AND HEALING (4:23–25)

These three verses amount to a summary statement of Jesus' public ministry. His travels throughout Galilee were characterized by preaching the gospel to open-air crowds as well as in local synagogues. Jesus' preaching was accompanied by mighty acts of healing.

■ *Jesus' invitation to repent, to receive the good*
■ *news, and to become citizens of God's kingdom*
■ *will have significant implications for the atti-*
■ *tudes and behavior of those who respond. We see*
■ *the details of kingdom living in what follows.*

## QUESTIONS TO GUIDE YOUR STUDY

1. How did Jesus' three temptations differ?
2. What can we learn from the way Jesus resisted and defended Himself against these attacks from the devil?
3. How will Jesus help you deal with temptations in your life?

## MATTHEW 5

This chapter begins Jesus' first of five discourses in Matthew. This discourse, known as the Sermon on the Mount, covers 5:3–7:27.

## THE SETTING (5:1–2)

This sermon likely took place on a plateau in a hilly area near the Sea of Galilee.

## THE BEATITUDES (5:3–12)

 Jesus presents His hearers with nine Beatitudes. These Beatitudes instruct followers of Jesus in how to have real and lasting happiness. The word *blessed* refers to those who are, and will be, happy because of God's response to their behavior or situation.

### *"Blessed are the poor in spirit, for theirs is the kingdom of God"* (v. 3)

These are people who realize their own spiritual poverty. They put all their trust in God's ability to supply their spiritual need.

### *"Blessed are those who mourn, for they will be comforted"* (v. 4)

Those who feel sorrowful because of their own sins and failure, and because of the world's evil will ultimately be comforted.

### *"Blessed are the meek, for they will inherit the earth"* (v. 5)

The meek person has "a gentle strength." (Robertson). God gave a Promised Land to His people in the Old Testament. The new land of promise will be inherited by those who manifest this characteristic.

"But the humble will inherit the land, and will delight themselves in abundant prosperity." (Ps. 37:11 NASB).

### *"Blessed are those who hunger and thirst for righteousness, for they will be filled"* (v. 6)

These are people who want, more than anything else, to see the world's evil (including what is wrong in their own lives) overcome by God's righteousness. Jesus promises these people that God's righteousness will prevail, and their desire for it will be satisfied.

### *"Blessed are the merciful, for they will be shown mercy" (v. 7)*

Merciful people realize their own need for God's pardon. Having known God's grace in their own lives, they want to forgive and help others.

### *"Blessed are the pure in heart, for they shall see God" (v. 8)*

The pure in heart are those who serve God with single-minded devotion and unmixed motives.

### *"Blessed are the peacemakers, for they will be called sons of God" (v. 9)*

"Let it be your ambition to live at peace with all men and to achieve holiness 'without which no man will see the Lord.'" (Heb. 12:14 PHILLIPS).

Jesus promises this blessing not to those who remained neutral, or to those who simply love peace, but to those who are actively involved in making peace. Christ Himself was the "Prince of Peace" (Isa. 9:6). He came to bring reconciliation between God and mankind and between individuals. Those who, through Him, are at peace with God can join Him in His work of reconciliation.

### *"Blessed are those who are persecuted because of righteousness, for theirs is the kingdom of heaven" (v. 10)*

Jesus declares that the kingdom of heaven belongs to those who are persecuted for upholding God's standards of justice, truth, and goodness.

### *"Blessed are you when people insult you, persecute you and falsely say all kinds of evil against you because of me" (v. 11)*

This is an expansion of the preceding beatitude, and is often included with it. Here Jesus tells the disciples that the consequences of following Him might result in persecution for righteousness' sake.

■ *Humanity's self-centeredness seeks personal*
■ *security and survival above the good of oth-*
■ *ers. The Beatitudes, the kingdom blessings,*
■ *are an inversion of that attitude and its*
■ *accompanying worldly value system.*

## SALT AND LIGHT (5:13–16)

Jesus teaches His disciples that their functions in the world are like those of salt and light.

### *"You are the salt of the earth" (vv. 13–14)*

Salt was important in the ancient world because it kept food from spoiling. Like food, society needs an antidote for its corruption. The disciples are to be this antidote.

### *"You are the light of the world" (vv. 14–16)*

Jesus Himself is the "true light" (John 1:9) and the "light of the world" (John 8:12). He then also called the disciples "the light of the world." They radiated the light that came from Him just as the lights of a city situated on a hilltop cannot be hidden.

■ *Both metaphors which Jesus uses in this sec-*
■ *tion raise important questions about Chris-*
■ *tian involvement in society. We are not*
■ *called to control secular power structures.*
■ *But we must remain active preservative*
■ *agents in calling the world to heed God's*
■ *standards.*

Salt is different from the food into which it is put. When a Christian stops being different from the world and no longer works against the forces of decay, that person stops being salt to the earth. Such a Christian will have no positive influence in the world.

A lamp that is hidden provides no benefit. Christians sometimes try to hide their light from the world's darkness. Instead, they are to shine in the darkness, dispelling the darkness with loving service. They are to make their influence as Christians felt in the world. Their motive is not to draw attention to themselves, but to lead people to give glory to God, who is the source of their works.

## THE PLACE OF THE JEWISH LAW (5:17–20)

Jesus tells His listeners that He has not come "to abolish the Law or the Prophets." Rather, He has come to fulfill them.

Jesus goes on to describe the kind of righteousness He requires of His followers by means of six illustrations seen in verses 21–48.

- *Jesus came not to abolish the Law and the*
- *Prophets, but to fulfill them and to make it*
- *possible for His followers to fulfill them.*

## A NEW LOOK AT THE LAW AGAINST MURDER (5:21–26)

After reminding His listeners that the Ten Commandments forbade murder, Jesus goes on to deepen the requirements of that commandment. He points out the attitudes of hatred, anger, and contempt that lay behind the act of murder. He considers those attitudes so seriously wrong that He suggests they should be punishable as the actual act of murder.

One who has contempt for another sees that person as less than completely human. Murder grows out of that attitude. Jesus provided two illustrations.

- *We are all on our way to God's court. Chris-*
- *tians should settle any differences with oth-*
- *ers in this life. Reconciliation with others*
- *shows a right relationship with God.*

## THE PROBLEMS OF ADULTERY AND DIVORCE (5:27–32)

### The Problem of Adultery (vv. 27–30)

Jesus next reinterprets the commandment forbidding adultery. He teaches that it is not enough simply to refrain from the act of adultery. Lust, too, is sinful and is the beginning point for actually committing adultery.

### The Problem of Divorce (vv. 31–32)

According to Jewish Law, a man could divorce his wife, but a wife could not divorce her husband. To give some protection to wives, the Law required a husband to provide the wife he was divorcing a "certificate of divorce."

■ *Jesus' words about marriage and divorce are*
■ *meant to reveal God's ideal standard—mar-*
■ *riage is a solemn, lifelong covenant between*
■ *a man and a woman.*

Jesus has a more exacting standard for His followers than what the Jewish Law demands. Jesus opposed divorce completely, except in the case of adultery.

## OATH TAKING (5:33–37)

An oath that made use of God's name was considered absolutely binding. For fear of not being able to keep a promise, a person might swear by something less than God's name, such as Jerusalem or the earth, for example. Jesus totally rejected this practice.

Jesus declared that everything was connected to God, and He told His followers not to take oaths. A person of integrity, one whose word can be trusted, has no need for oaths.

## HOW TO OVERCOME EVIL (5:38–42)

Jesus quotes part of the Old Testament Law of retaliation (Lev. 24:17–20). But He teaches that

His followers are to live by a higher standard than that. They are not to "resist" evil with evil. Instead, if they are struck on one cheek, they are to "turn the other cheek." Turning the other cheek could mean to act in a positive way for the good of the one who has given the insult.

 In dealing with others, Jesus teaches that His followers should be willing to give more than the Law requires. If forced to walk one mile by someone, a Christian ought to travel voluntarily *two* miles with that person.

- *Jesus teaches His disciples to let generosity,*
- *not the desire for revenge, rule their relation-*
- *ships with others. A Christian should be will-*
- *ing to do more than forced to do.*

## HOW TO TREAT AN ENEMY (5:43–48)

Jesus opposes an attitude of hatred for one's enemies. He calls for love for one's enemies and prayer for one's persecutors. To act in such a way would be to exhibit some of the same characteristics of God Himself.

There is nothing unusual about loving someone who loves us back. But it takes grace to love those who hate us. Jesus' followers must demonstrate this higher moral standard.

- *Christians are to be good to all people,*
- *including their enemies.*

## QUESTIONS TO GUIDE YOUR STUDY

1. What was the significance of the Sermon on the Mount? Does it have a present-day application?
2. Jesus used salt and light to describe how His disciples should function in the world. In what ways do His disciples function as salt and light?
3. What was Jesus' position on divorce? How does society's standard measure up to His standard?

## MATTHEW 6

This chapter is a continuation of the Sermon on the Mount.

### FIRST EXAMPLE: HOW TO GIVE GIFTS (6:2–4)

Almsgiving was the practice of giving charitable gifts. Because Jewish Law did not require almsgiving, it was considered especially praiseworthy. "Sounding the trumpet" was a figurative way of saying that the people of Jesus' day found ways of calling others' attention to what they were doing.

■ *Jesus does not want His disciples to do good*
■ *works in order to bring attention to them-*
■ *selves. God sees all gifts, even those given in*
■ *secret.*

## SECOND EXAMPLE: THE MODEL PRAYER (6:6–15)

### Its Purpose and Structure

In teaching the disciples about prayer, Jesus contrasts the insincere prayers of hypocrites with the proper way to pray. So He provides them with a model prayer. This prayer is also known as the "The Lord's Prayer" or "The Disciple's Prayer." It is a model prayer because it contains the components and attitudes that Jesus' disciples should exhibit and incorporate into their lives. The first half of this prayer focuses exclusively on God and His agenda as believers adore, worship, and submit to His will before they introduce their own personal petitions.

### Its Petitions

### *"Our Father in heaven" (v. 9)*

Jesus knew God as His Father, and He taught the disciples to trust Him as their Father. The phrase "in heaven" balances this intimacy with an affirmation of God's sovereignty and majesty.

**Father**

Jesus addressed God as "Father," which translates the Aramaic word *Abba*. It is an intimate term, and its use in this way was unparalleled in first-century Judaism. God is as accessible as the most loving human parent.

### *"Hallowed be your name" (v. 9)*

In Hebrew thought, one's name represented that person's personality, character, and authority. This first petition is a plea that all people may come to regard God as holy. We should treat all that God has created as holy and honored because of His perfection and goodness.

### *"Your kingdom come, your will be done" (v. 10)*

These two petitions are closely related and have almost the same meaning. They express the desire that the acknowledgment of God's reign and the accomplishment of His purposes take place in the world even as they already do in heaven. This request is that victory over evil will become a reality.

### "Give us today our daily bread" (v. 11)

From this point on, the prayer's petitions have to do with peoples' needs. Jesus recognizes that His followers need food and other essentials. "Daily" means that which is necessary for existence for the immediate future, perhaps for the coming day. This part of the prayer acknowledges our ultimate dependence on God's generosity for all our needs. Christians, therefore, should pray daily for the next day's provision of life's essentials as they recognize that all sustenance for life comes from God.

"The meaning . . . seems to be 'for the coming day.'"
A.T. Robertson, *WPNT*, I, 53.

### "Forgive us our debts, as we also have forgiven our debtors" (v. 12)

His petition sees us as debtors before God because of our sins. It is a plea for continued forgiveness, requesting the restoration of fellowship with God. At the same time it acknowledges that we cannot expect to receive God's forgiveness unless we show forgiveness toward those who have wronged us.

Temptation

When people are tempted, they should not say, 'God is tempting me."

Evil cannot tempt God, and God himself does not tempt anyone" (James 1:13, NCV).

### "Lead us not into temptation, but deliver us from the evil one" (v. 13)

Whereas the previous petition asked forgiveness for sins one has committed, this petition asks for strength *not* to commit future sins. We must be careful not to misunderstand this request to mean that God brings us to the place of temptation. The best way we should take these words is, "Don't let us succumb to temptation," or "Don't abandon us to temptation." The second part of this petition is a plea for deliverance from the "evil one," Satan, from whom all evil ultimately comes.

## AN ADDITIONAL NOTE (6:14–15)

These two verses contain an explanation of prayer for forgiveness of sins, and describes the negative consequences of failure to forgive others. The person who does not forgive will not be forgiven.

■ *The Model Prayer contains the components*
■ *and attitudes that Jesus' disciples should*
■ *exhibit and incorporate into their lives.*

## THIRD EXAMPLE: FASTING (6:16–18)

Fasting, or abstinence from food for a period of time, is the third religious practice Jesus warned about. Like almsgiving and prayer, fasting must come from the right motive or it loses its value. Jesus declares that the hypocrites made a conspicuous production of their fasting. They did so to gain praise from people rather than from God.

Jesus wants His disciples to behave differently. They are to behave normally when they fast, knowing that God alone would know about their secret act of devotion.

■ *Fasting was the third religious practice Jesus*
■ *warned His disciples about. The key to the*
■ *religious practice of fasting is doing it with*
■ *the right motive.*

## TRUE AND LASTING RICHES (6:19–21)

Jesus wanted people to have life's material necessities. But He knew the dangers of making the accumulation of material possessions the

**Fasting**

Fasting is the laying aside of food for a period of time when a believer is seeking to know God in a deeper experience. The Bible describes three main forms of fasting: (1) the normal fast—abstinence from food; (2) the absolute fast—abstinence from both food and water; and (3) the partial fast—a restriction of diet rather than complete abstinence.

goal of one's life. He taught that there is no final security in earthly possessions. People need, instead, to devote their attention to acquiring "treasures in heaven."

**Treasures in Heaven**

This phrase can be defined broadly as holiness of character, obedience to all of God's commands, service to God, and merciful deeds done to others. In this context, however, storing up spiritual treasures focuses particularly on the compassionate use of material resources to meet the physical and spiritual needs of others, in keeping with kingdom priorities.

- *Rather than accumulating material wealth,*
- *Jesus' followers will work for spiritual riches*
- *that are invulnerable to loss and death.*

## THE LAMP AND THE BODY (6:22–23)

Jesus draws a spiritual analogy from the physical realm. The physical eye brings light or darkness into the body, depending on the eye's state of health. A person's inner being, too, has an eye—a spiritual eye that is focused on God. If that eye is sound, it brings God's light into the person's being. However, if the eye tries to focus on both God and worldly values at the same time, it becomes unsound. Spiritual vision then becomes blurred, and spiritual darkness instead of light will fill the person.

- *The health of one's spiritual eye determines*
- *one's overall well-being.*

## THE CHOICE OF A MASTER (6:24)

Jesus teaches that no one can be a slave to two masters. *Mammon* is the Aramaic word meaning "money" or "material resources." Many perceptive observers have sensed that the greatest danger to Western Christianity is not prevailing ideologies or philosophies, but the all-pervasive materialism of our affluent culture.

25

- *Serving God demands full allegiance. The*
- *pursuit of wealth can be all-absorbing, leav-*
- *ing no room for God in our lives.*

## THE FUTILITY OF WORRY (6:25–33)

*Worry* is the key word of this section, as it occurs six times. Certainly Christians must plan for the future, but they need not be anxious. Jesus illustrates His point by discussing the basic provisions of food and clothing. God provides for the birds of the air and the lilies of the field. In view of God's provision, anxiety over food, clothing, and the future is pagan.

- *Those who make service to God their life's*
- *goal need not worry about material provi-*
- *sions.*

## QUESTIONS TO GUIDE YOUR STUDY

1. Name the three illustrations of piety Jesus used. What point was He making with these?
2. How can we best make use of the Model Prayer?
3. What is the danger of focusing on acquiring material possessions in this life?

## JUDGMENT AND DISCERNMENT (7:1–6)

Jesus warns that His disciples are not to be characterized by judgmental attitudes. Certainly, some kinds of judgment are necessary, but Jesus warns against unloving, condemning criticism of another person. On those occasions when we render a negative evaluation of others, our purposes should be constructive and not retributive. The lesson of this parable is that we must not presume to judge others.

## PRAYER: ASKING, SEEKING, KNOCKING (7:7–12)

### Persistence in Prayer (vv. 7–11)

Jesus teaches that His disciples should pray persistently. The verbs *ask, seek,* and *knock* are present imperative forms that stress the need for persistence, often over a period of time. This persistence is an indication of our seriousness in making the request and of our confidence that God will answer. It is petitioning God with an expectant attitude.

A key theme here is God's generosity. Jesus says that if human parents who are sinful know how to give good gifts to their children, how much more will God, who is perfect, give good gifts to those who ask.

■ *Persistent prayer brings an answer. God is*
■ *generous and gives only good gifts to those*
■ *who come to Him in prayer.*

Judge

This word can imply "to analyze or evaluate" as well as "to condemn or avenge." The former senses are clearly commended to believers (e.g., 1 Cor. 5:5; 1 John 4:1), but the latter are reserved for God. In this passage, the word is used to forbid an action already taking place and can be translated as "stop judging."

**The Golden Rule**

This name is usually given to the command of Jesus recorded here and in Luke 6:31. The designation "Golden Rule" does not appear in the Bible, and its origin in English is difficult to trace. The principle of the Golden Rule can be found in many religions, but Jesus' wording of it was original and unique.

### The Golden Rule (v. 12)

"In everything, do to others what you would have them do to you." This saying has become known as the Golden Rule because of its central role in Christian ethics. It was known to the Jews in a negative form, but Jesus gave it a positive turn. Note that this rule is meant for those under the rule of God, not for the world at large. Only a person whose will is submitted to God can care as much about another's welfare as his own.

■ *In view of God's generosity to us, treating*
■ *others in the manner we would like to be*
■ *treated ourselves is the least we can do.*

The rest of the Sermon on the Mount offers no new commandments, but encourages obedience to those already given while warning against disobedience. The following three illustrations by Jesus make plain that there are ultimately only two categories of people in the world: (1) Those who hear, obey, and are saved and, (2) those who only hear, and so are destroyed. In each case, the consequences are eternal.

### THE WIDE AND NARROW GATES (7:13–14)

This first illustration contrasts those who select the narrow rather than the wide gate. Jesus teaches that there are two differing paths a person may follow as seen in Psalm 1. Most people, with little thought, enter the wide gate and follow the easy, wide way. It takes a definite, conscious act of the will to choose the narrow gate and follow the diffi-

**"Narrow" — "Broad"**

The word *narrow* comes from a verb meaning "to experience trouble or difficulty"; whereas *broad* can have overtones of "prosperous."

cult narrow way. The hard, narrow way leads, in the end, to life for the few who find it.

## THE TRUE AND THE FALSE (7:15–23)

The second illustration contrasts those who bear good fruit with those who bear bad fruit. Jesus knew that, at times, His Church would be influenced by false prophets. His followers needed to be able to distinguish between the true and the false. Jesus gave only one criterion: fruit.

## THE PARABLE OF THE TWO BUILDERS (7:24–27)

The third illustration contrasts those who build their homes on solid rock with those who build on shifting sand. The foolish person would build directly on the sand and have no protection against the devastation of the elements.

A wise person building in the Palestinian desert would erect a dwelling on a secure rock to protect the house from flash floods.

- *It is not enough simply to hear Jesus' call or*
- *even to respond with a flurry of good deeds.*
- *Rather, we must build a solid foundation that*
- *combines authentic commitment to Christ*
- *with persevering obedience.*

## THE CROWD'S RESPONSE TO JESUS (7:28–29)

Jesus spoke with a power and authority that commanded the attention and respect of His listeners. The crowds marveled and contrasted Jesus' teaching with that of the scribes. For the people, the difference was one of authority.

## QUESTIONS TO GUIDE YOUR STUDY

1. What principles of prayer did Jesus teach?

2. What are some ways we might apply the Golden Rule in our everyday lives?

3. What lessons can we draw from Jesus' three illustrations about disobedience?

## MATTHEW 8

### JESUS' HEALING OF A LEPER (8:1–4)

Following the Sermon on the Mount, as Jesus descended the mountain, a leper came and knelt before Him and said, "Lord, if you are willing, you can make me clean." This was an opportunity for Jesus to show how He viewed the Law. The leper's coming to Jesus was in itself a violation of the Law of Moses, since lepers were considered unclean. Jesus reached out and touched the leper, healing him immediately. Because the Law forbade touching a leper, this gesture proved at least as shocking as the leper's original approach and request. But Jesus' touch makes clean what was unclean. Of interest is the fact that Jesus sent the man to the priest in accordance with the requirements of Lev. 14:1–32. Jesus honors the Law of Moses, teaches others to do so, but gives a glimpse, in this healing, of what it means to fulfill the Law.

### THE HEALING OF THE CENTURION'S SERVANT (8:5–13)

As Jesus reached Capernaum, the headquarters for His Galilean ministry, a centurion met Him, asking for help. This centurion was a Gentile officer in the Roman army. He explained to Jesus that his servant was paralyzed and "in terrible suffering." Orthodox Jews would have considered the centurion unclean because of his

**Leprosy**

*Leprosy* was a generic term applied to a variety of skin disorders, ranging from psoriasis to leprosy. Its symptoms ranged from white patches on the skin to running sores to the loss of fingers and toes. For the Hebrews, it was a dreaded malady that rendered its victims ceremonially unclean—unfit to worship God. In addition, anyone who came in contact with a leper was considered unclean.

race and would have despised him all the more as a symbol of Roman oppression.

The centurion's faith in Jesus was strong: "Just say the word, and my servant will be healed." Jesus was amazed at his faith. It even exceeded the faith He had found among God's own people, the Jews. In response to the centurion's faith, Jesus told the man that his request was answered. At that moment, the centurion's servant was healed.

## THE HEALING OF SIMON PETER'S MOTHER-IN-LAW (8:14–15)

Simon Peter had a house in Capernaum. When Jesus visited Peter's home, He saw that Peter's mother-in-law was "lying in bed with a fever." She may have had malaria. Jesus healed the woman by touching her hand. Her fever left and her strength returned immediately. She began serving Jesus, who was a guest in the house.

This small miracle highlights at least three important points:

1. It shows Jesus healing a woman.
2. The healing was a privately done miracle.
3. It shows that a person who has been touched by Jesus, whether physically or spiritually, will want to serve Him.

## OTHER HEALINGS (8:16–17)

That same night, Jesus healed many others who were brought to Him.

Matthew wrote that these healings fulfilled Isaiah's prophecy in Isa. 53:4: "He took up our infirmities and carried our sorrows."

■ *The three miracles recorded in this chapter*
■ *demonstrate Jesus' willingness to become*
■ *unclean in order to make others clean.*

## TWO WHO WANTED TO FOLLOW JESUS (8:18–22)

As Jesus planned to cross to the other side of the Sea of Galilee to escape the crowds, two would-be followers spoke to Him.

### *The Scribe (vv. 18–20)*

The scribe was overly eager to become a disciple. He assured Jesus that he would follow Him anywhere He might go. Jesus recognized that in his confident enthusiasm, the scribe had failed to grasp what following Jesus might involve. In Jesus' response to the scribe, He refers to Himself as the Son of Man.

### *A Would-Be Disciple (vv. 21–22)*

Whereas the scribe was overly eager, this man was hesitant. He wanted to follow Jesus, but only after he had taken care of other obligations. He was not ready to follow Jesus, as other priorities came before discipleship.

■ *Discipleship involves commitment and sacri-*
■ *fice. Those who would be disciples need to*
■ *count the cost.*

## JESUS' CALMING OF THE STORM (8:23–27)

Jesus and His disciples boarded a boat for the trip across the Sea of Galilee. Jesus slept during the crossing. A sudden storm arose, and the waves began to engulf the boat. Lives were at risk! Amazingly, Jesus remained so calm that He continued to sleep. His frightened disciples awakened Him, begging Him to save them from the storm's danger. Jesus chided them for their fear and lack of belief. Then He stood and

Storms on the Sea of Galilee

Such storms are the result of two simple facts:
1. Water retains its warmth longer than the surrounding land, and
2. The warm air above the lake tends to rise whereas cold air sinks. When the sides of the lake are steep, this movement of the air is exaggerated. The cold air pours down the hillside like a flood, suddenly displacing the warmer air, which is forced upward.
Denis Baly

calmed the waves and wind. The disciples wondered aloud about the identity of the Man: "What kind of man is this? Even the winds and the waves obey him."

- *Jesus demonstrated power over the destruc-*
- *tive forces of nature, which were under the*
- *devil's sway. Such a Person is worthy of wor-*
- *ship.*

## JESUS' HEALING OF TWO DEMON-POSSESSED MEN (8:28–34)

Here Matthew's narrative illustrates Jesus' ministry of exorcism. When Jesus and His disciples arrived on the eastern side of the Sea of Galilee, they were met by two demon-possessed men. These mentally deranged men lived in tombs, or burial caves, in the side of a mountain. These men were so violent that no one would go near them.

The demons possessing these men recognized Jesus and His power to destroy them. When they realized that Jesus intended to cast them out of the men, they asked to be sent to a herd of pigs nearby. Swine, like tombs, were sources of defilement according the the Law of Moses. Jesus agreed to their request.

When the demons entered the pigs, the entire herd rushed down the steep bank and drowned in the Sea of Galilee. This demonstrated Jesus' authority over the forces of evil. The local farmers and townsfolk asked Jesus to leave, as His presence made them uncomfortable.

"The whole subject of demonology is difficult. Some hold that it is only the ancient way of describing disease. But that does not explain the situation here. Jesus is represented as treating the demons as really existing as separate from the human personality." A.T. Robertson, *WPNT*, I, 69.

■ *Jesus demonstrated His authority over the*
■ *powers of evil. The local people asked Jesus*
■ *to leave their area. Sinful people often recoil*
■ *in the presence of holiness because it high-*
■ *lights their own shortcomings and, in this*
■ *case, had negative economic implications.*

## QUESTIONS TO GUIDE YOUR STUDY

1. Jesus' miracles in this chapter demonstrate His authority. What was significant about each miracle with regard to the positioning of the Jewish Law?
2. What does Jesus require of those who follow Him?
3. Have you had experiences that prompted you to express awe at the character or attributes of God?

**Son of Man**

Matthew uses this term to express the deity of Jesus, the unique Son of God. His references point to some aspect of Jesus' earthly ministry, such as His authority to forgive sins and to interpret the meaning of the Sabbath. Three categories of "Son of Man" sayings in the Gospels are generally recognized: (1) those that present Him in His earthly role, (2) those that highlight His suffering, and (3) those that point to His glory. The background for this title is likely Dan. 7:13–14.

# MATTHEW 9

## A PARALYTIC'S FORGIVENESS AND HEALING (9:1–8)

After Jesus returned to Capernaum, a group of men brought a paralytic to Jesus for healing. Surprisingly, Jesus declared the man's sins forgiven. Apparently, Jesus had decided that such forgiveness was necessary before the paralytic could be healed. In response to the faith of those who brought this man, Jesus both forgave the man's sins and healed him. The crowd was amazed at Jesus, with a combination of terror and awe, and they gave glory to God for what He had done.

- *This miracle caused people to give glory to*
- *God because He had delegated such author-*
- *ity to Jesus. His works of healing and forgiv-*
- *ing were signs that God's kingdom was*
- *dawning.*

### THE CALL OF MATTHEW (9:9–13)

#### Matthew Becomes a Disciple (v. 9)
Passing by the customs house (toll station) in Capernaum, Jesus saw Matthew, a Jewish tax collector. Tax collectors were an especially despised group of people, with corruption widespread in their ranks. Matthew gives no indication of any prior exposure to Jesus' person or preaching. When Jesus called Matthew to follow Him As a disciple, Matthew responded immediately.

#### Matthew Throws a Party (vv. 10–11)
On a later occasion, Matthew threw a party for Jesus. Many of Matthew's colleagues, fellow tax collectors, and other "sinners" joined him.

#### The Pharisees' Criticism (vv. 11–13)
The Pharisees could not understand why Jesus would eat with the kinds of people who attended Matthew's party. Contact with "sinners" was forbidden by their laws. Consequently, they questioned the disciples about Jesus' behavior. Jesus, however, heard their questioning and answered them Himself. He replied, "It is not the healthy who need a doctor, but the sick." He had come to call sinners, not the righteous. He suggested that the Pharisees study Hos. 6:6: "I desire mercy, not sacrifice." The Pharisees had become so intent on the

Matthew

*Matthew* means "the gift of God." He was a tax collector called by Jesus to be an apostle. Why did Jesus call Matthew? Because Matthew had the gifts to be trained as a disciple to share with others, could keep meticulous records, and was a potential recorder-author of the Gospel of Matthew. From the earliest times, Christians have affirmed that Matthew wrote the Gospel that bears his name.

The NIV puts the word "sinners" in quotation marks because the term was used in at least two special senses. Here, the term refers to the most criminal and disreputable kinds of people in society.

perfect keeping of their rituals that they neglected showing mercy to others.

■ *Jesus' fraternizing with disreputable people*
■ *provided an example for His disciples. We*
■ *would do well to reevaluate regularly our*
■ *efforts to reach those in need and those con-*
■ *sidered outcasts in our society.*

## A QUESTION ABOUT FASTING (9:14–17)

### *John's Disciples Raise the Question (v. 14)*

Some disciples of John the Baptist came to Jesus with a question. Both they and the Pharisees fasted, but Jesus and His disciples did not make a practice of doing so. John's disciples wanted to know why.

Jesus had no objections to fasting, and at times, fasted Himself (Matt. 4:2). He believed, however, that a person should fast only when the occasion warranted it and not as a mechanical ritual.

The parable of the bridegroom (v. 15). In the Old Testament, fasting was usually a spontaneous expression of mourning, repentance, or supplication in a time of crisis. Jesus used this opportunity to refer to His coming death. "Will be taken away" perhaps alludes to Isa. 53:8 and a foreshadowing of Jesus' crucifixion. At that point, fasting and mourning will be appropriate.

### *Jesus' Answer (vv. 15–16)*

Jesus provided an illustration of the fact that existing religious structures of His day could not contain the new wine of His gospel.

### *Illustration of New Wine into Old Wineskins (vv. 16–17).*

Jesus reinforced His point of the parable by illustrating the incompatibility of the old and the new ages. A person would be foolish to place an unshrunk patch of cloth on an old garment. It would pull and tear at the garment. Nor would someone pour new wine into a brittle old wineskin. The fermenting of the wine would eventually cause the wineskin to burst. A person should use new containers that are flexible.

■ *Judaism's emphasis on legalism and rituals*
■ *was incompatible with Jesus' gospel.*

## FOUR DIFFERENT MIRACLES (9:18–34)

Matthew's narrative now presents a group of four healings. Jesus' activities are beginning to attract the opposition of Jewish leaders.

### A Request to Raise a Daughter (vv. 18–19)

A ruler of the synagogue asked Jesus to heal his daughter, who had "just died." From the accounts of Mark and Luke we know this ruler's name was Jairus. This man believed strongly in Jesus' power over death. Jesus and His disciples went with Jairus.

### Miracle One: The Healing of a Woman with a Long-Term Illness (vv. 20–22)

On their way to Jairus's house, a woman came behind Jesus and touched the edge of His cloak. She had experienced hemorrhaging for twelve years. She believed she could be healed if only she could touch Jesus' clothing. At that moment Jesus turned, looked at the woman, and declared that her faith had brought healing.

### Miracle Two: The Raising of the Ruler's Daughter (vv. 23–26)

Jesus then completed His trip to Jairus's house. Upon arriving, He ordered the musicians and professional mourners to leave. Jesus viewed the girl's death as temporary. He took the girl's hand, lifted her up, and brought her back to life. The news of this miracle spread like wildfire.

"When you are sick, offer to Christ all your pains, your suffering and your listlessness. Ask him to unite them to those he bore for you. Obey your doctor, take your medicine, your food and your remedies for love of God remembering how he tasted gall for love of mankind. Desire to recover in order to serve him, but be prepared to suffer on in obedience to his will, and prepare to die when he calls you, that you may be with him and praise His name forever."

Francis de Sales, *Joy of the Saints,* (Springfield: Templegate Publishers, 1988), p. 329.

**"According to Your Faith"**

This phrase means "in response to," not "in proportion to" their faith.

### Miracle Three: The Restoring of Two Blind Men's Sight (vv. 27–31)

Jesus next demonstrated His healing power over blindness. Two blind men called out to Him and begged for healing. Jesus first made certain they believed He could heal them. He told them, "According to your faith will it be done to you." In response to their faith, He gave them their sight.

### Miracle Four: The Healing of a Mute (vv. 32–34)

A demon-possessed man who couldn't talk was brought to Jesus for healing. This man's illness cut him off from society. Jesus cast out the demon, and to the amazement of the onlookers, the man was able to speak.

■ *These miracles show the relationship*
■ *between faith and miracles.*

### JESUS' REASON FOR MINISTRY (9:35–38)

Jesus had deep compassion for the crowds. He likened them to sheep without a shepherd, and as a vast crop of ripe grain in need of harvesters. He decided it was time to send out laborers to gather the harvest. In this section, Matthew lists the twelve disciples called to join Jesus in His mission.

### QUESTIONS TO GUIDE YOUR STUDY

1. Explain the significance of fasting. What are its benefits? How should one practice fasting?

2. Why couldn't the Pharisees' religion receive Jesus' gospel?

3. What was the driving force behind Jesus' ministry?

## MATTHEW 10 - - - - - - - - - - - - - - - -

### A LISTING OF THE TWELVE (10:1–4)

Jesus called twelve men to be His apostles. Their number calls to mind the twelve tribes of Israel and suggests that Jesus was building a community of followers in conscious opposition to the current leadership of Israel.

 *The Twelve Apostles*

| NAME | MEANING OF NAME |
|------|------------------|
| Simon | "hearing" (Hebrew) |
| Andrew | "manliness" (Greek) |
| James | "Jacob" (Hebrew) |
| John | "the Lord is gracious" (Hebrew) |
| Philip | "horse lover" (Greek) |
| Bartholomew | "son of Talmai" (Hebrew) |
| Thomas | "twin" (Hebrew) |
| Matthew | "God has given" (Hebrew) |
| James "the younger" | "Jacob" (Hebrew); "the small one" |
| Thaddaeus | from "breast" and "heart" (Hebrew) |
| Simon the Zealot | "zealous one" (Greek) |
| Judas Iscariot | "man of Kerioth" (Hebrew) |

- *The twelve men Jesus chose to represent Him*
- *were not likely the kind we would have cho-*
- *sen for an important mission. Yet Jesus*

**Apostle**

Apostles were persons sent to accomplish a mission, especially the twelve apostles Jesus commissioned to follow him. An apostle represents the one sending and has authority to represent the sender in business, political, or educational situations.

■ *granted them authority to do miracles and*
■ *relied on them to be His first laborers in the*
■ *field.*

## THE APOSTLES' ASSIGNMENT (10:5–15)

Jesus sent the twelve disciples on a special mission. According to Mark's Gospel, He sent them out in pairs. This mission included preaching the gospel, healing the sick, and exorcising demons. He told the Twelve to concentrate on the "lost sheep of Israel." Jesus provided specific instructions for carrying out the mission.

■ *Israel would be the first to receive the gospel*
■ *message.*

## WARNINGS AND ASSURANCES ABOUT PERSECUTION (10:16–33)

### *Jesus Warns Them of Possible Persecution (vv. 16–28 )*

Jesus declared that He was sending out His apostles as "sheep among wolves" (v. 16). They would be faced with possible persecution from civil and religious authorities for representing Jesus. However, their proper response was to fear God, not people.

Verses 22 and 23 are two of Jesus' most difficult sayings to interpret. Their meanings are not certain.

*Saying One:* "He who stands firm to the end will be saved." He could have meant that a person dying for Christ or denying Him would be vindicated by God if he chose to be loyal unto death.

*Saying Two:* "You will not finish going through the cities of Israel before the Son of Man comes." Jesus was referring to something other than the final appearing of the Son of Man at the end of the age. The transfiguration of Jesus is one possibility. Or, He may have been speaking of the times He would appear after His resurrection.

### Jesus Reassures Them of God's Love
(vv. 29–33)

God had even counted the hairs on their heads! The disciples were of great value to God. Those who would acknowledge Jesus before others would receive acknowledgment by Jesus to God the Father. To "acknowledge" Jesus means to declare one's allegiance to Him. It carries the sense of "confess" or "trust in."

■ *The disciples would be faced with possible per-*
■ *secution from civil and religious authorities for*
■ *representing Jesus. He taught them that their*
■ *proper response was to fear God, not people.*

### PUTTING GOD ABOVE FAMILY
(10:34–39)

Jesus declared that anyone who loved a family member more than Him was not worthy of Him. Jesus must take first place in the life of a follower, who must "take his cross and follow" Jesus. To carry one's cross means a willingness to die for Jesus.

■ *Jesus was on the way to a cross, and His fol-*
■ *lowers had to be ready to share His death, if*
■ *necessary.*

## REWARDS FOR RECEIVING GOD'S MESSENGERS (10:40–11:1)

The people's reception of the Apostles would correspond to their reception of Jesus. Those who received the Apostles would be receiving Jesus and the Father. Those who received any messenger of Jesus would be rewarded.

Jesus' instructions to the twelve apostles about their mission was now complete. He closed His discourse on an optimistic note in hopes of a positive response.

## QUESTIONS TO GUIDE YOUR STUDY

1. Describe your initial impressions about the twelve men whom Jesus called to be His apostles. How do they complement each other? What potential personnel management issues might Jesus face?

2. What was the purpose of Jesus' assignment for the disciples?

3. Explain Jesus' insistence on placing the importance of discipleship above that of the family.

# MATTHEW 11 · · · · · · · · · · · · · · · · · · ·

Verse 1 can be taken as a conclusion to the previous sermon in chapter 10, or as a transitional verse. At this time, Jesus carried on His ministry of teaching and preaching in the towns and villages of Galilee.

## A QUESTION FROM JOHN THE BAPTIST (11:2–6)

John the Baptist abruptly reappears in the narrative. He had been in prison during Jesus' Galilean ministry.

### John's Question about Jesus' Messiahship (vv. 2–3)

While in prison, John had heard some puzzling information about Jesus' ministry. Apparently, he was seeing no signs of the imminent judgment of the wicked that Jesus had promised (Matt. 3:10). John was beginning to have doubts about whether Jesus was the Messiah. As a result, he sent some of his disciples to question Jesus about His identity.

Even the most courageous and faithful of God's servants may experience doubt. Confessing our doubts to God and asking for His help is a good first step of faith.

### Jesus' Reply (vv. 4–6)

Jesus answered John's question by itemizing His works that authenticated His messiahship. He then encouraged John to remain faithful to Him, no matter what might come.

■ *John was beginning to doubt Jesus' identity.*
■ *His messiahship unfolded much differently*
■ *than most people expected it would—even*
■ *the most faithful. Most anticipated a political*
■ *leader who would overthrow the oppressing*
■ *Roman rule. Jesus assured John that He was*
■ *the Messiah and, in spite of appearances to*
■ *the contrary, He encouraged John to remain*
■ *faithful to Him.*

According to Jewish historian Josephus, Herod Antipas had John imprisoned in the fortress of Marchaerus, near the Dead Sea.

### JESUS' TESTIMONY ABOUT JOHN (11:7–15)

After answering John's question, Jesus talked to the crowds about John. He supported the legitimacy of John's ministry by posing two rhetorical questions:

1. Did they expect to see "a reed swaying in the wind"?

2. Did they expect to see a "man dressed in fine clothes"?

Jesus assured the crowd that John was God's messenger and that no person ever born was greater than John.

■ *Jesus confirmed the validity of John the Baptist's ministry and of John's greatness.*

## THE CROWDS' REACTION TO JESUS AND JOHN THE BAPTIST (11:16–19)

Jesus compared His own generation to children who criticized their friends for not playing games *their* way.

He then contrasted Himself with John. They were opposites in attitude and lifestyle, but both were necessary to God's plan.

## JUDGMENT ON UNBELIEVING TOWNS (11:20–24)

Although Jesus' mission was not to act primarily as a judge, He showed that judgment was part of His role. He functioned as judge when He condemned the cities that had rejected Him. He would judge a few cities more severely because they had received more immediate, dramatic, and straightforward revelation. He had special words of condemnation for Capernaum, where He had lived during His Galilean ministry.

## AN INVITATION FROM JESUS (11:25–30)

Jesus closed this time with the crowd with three important statements concerning the mystery of God's revelation, the source of His own authority, and an invitation to respond to the revelation they had so far received.

**Capernaum**

Capernaum appears in the biblical record only in the Gospels, where it is mentioned 16 times. Jesus chose Capernaum as His base of operations when He began His ministry (Mark 1:21; 2:1).

### The Mystery of God's Revelation (vv. 25–26)

These verses are apparently a public prayer. Jesus contrasted the "wise and learned" and the "little children." Little children were those who responded to God and saw Him at work in the ministry of Jesus. The wise and learned were people like the scribes and Pharisees who felt secure in their own knowledge and so failed to see God revealed in Jesus.

### The Source of Jesus' Authority (v. 27)

Jesus declared that God had committed "all things" to Him. God, therefore, was the source of His authority. The word used for "know" involves the most intimate and fullest acquaintance.

### The Invitation (vv. 28–30)

Jesus then appealed for a response to His revelation. It is an invitation to all who hurt or who recognize their spiritual need. He assured them that His "yoke was easy" and His "burden light." Jesus' requirements for righteousness were no less stringent than those of the Jewish leaders, but they could be accomplished more readily through the strength that Christ provides through the Holy Spirit.

Jesus equated the Christian life with rest. This rest would not be a life free from effort or sorrow. It would be a life of peace in the midst of life's trials and struggles. To illustrate this point, Jesus used a picture taken from farming. Like the yoke that couples oxen together, discipleship does not exempt one from work, but makes it manageable.

**Yoke**

A yoke was a wooden frame placed on draft animals to make them pull in tandem. Simple yokes consisted of a bar with two loops, either of rope or wood, which went around the animals' necks. In the Bible, the word *yoke* is most often used to speak of slavery, bondage, and hardship. Positive usages include the yoke of Christ (Matt. 11:29–30) and the joint nature of the Church's work (Phil. 4:3).

■ *Jesus delivered three commands in His invi-*
■ *tation: come, take, and learn. The first two*
■ *commands are in response to a crisis, but the*
■ *third is a response to "learn," and begins a*
■ *lifelong process of knowing God.*

## QUESTIONS TO GUIDE YOUR STUDY

1.  John the Baptist had prepared the way for Jesus. What circumstances caused him to now question Jesus' identity?
2.  Although they were quite different individuals, how did John the Baptist and Jesus complement each other? What did each uniquely accomplish?
3.  What truths might we derive from Jesus' actions against the cities that rejected Him?

The Sabbath is the day of rest, considered holy to God. Humans are to rest as God rested on the seventh day following the creation of the universe. It was viewed as a sign of the covenant relation between God and His people and of the eternal rest He promised them. The habit of Jesus was to observe the Sabbath as a day of worship in the synagogues, but His failure to comply with the minute restrictions brought conflict with the religious leaders of His day.

# MATTHEW 12

Sabbath observance was one of the three most important and distinctive badges of Jewish life (the other two were circumcision and dietary law).

## "REAPING" AND "THRESHING" ON THE SABBATH (12:1–8)

According to the laws of the scribes and Pharisees, it was lawful to satisfy one's hunger from a neighbor's grain field, but it was not lawful to do so on the Sabbath. The Pharisees observed what Jesus had done and reminded Him that His actions violated the Law. They viewed plucking grain as "reaping" and rubbing off the husks as "threshing." They classified these actions as "work."

Jesus responded to their objections by quoting examples from the Old Testament that showed human need was allowed to take precedence over religious regulations. Jesus climaxed the dialogue by stating, "The Son of Man is the Lord of the Sabbath" (v. 8). Jesus' sovereign authority would determine how the Sabbath is fulfilled in the kingdom age.

## HEALING ON THE SABBATH (12:9–14)

On the same day, Jesus went into a synagogue where He met a man with a shriveled hand. Taking the initiative to stir up controversy, the Pharisees posed this question to Jesus: "Is it lawful to heal on the Sabbath?" (v. 9).

Jesus first answered with a short parable about rescuing a sheep that had fallen into a pit. Sheep were valuable resources and exceptions were made for working to rescue sheep on a Sabbath. With one statement Jesus indicted the Pharisees' scale of values: "How much more valuable is a man than a sheep!" His conclusion was, "Therefore it is lawful to do good on the Sabbath" (v. 12). Jesus then healed the disabled man.

The Pharisees' power and influence came from the scrupulous keeping of the oral traditions. Jesus was a threat to all they stood for. For the first time in Matthew's Gospel, we are told that the Pharisees began to plot Jesus' death.

- As Messiah, the inaugurator of God's new
- age, Jesus had the right to reinterpret the
- Sabbath's meaning and requirements.

At this point, Matthew views Jesus' withdrawal as fulfillment of Isa. 42:1–4, depicting God's Suffering Servant. That passage predicted that God's servant would bring justice, but not by force or violence.

## JESUS WITHDRAWS FROM HOSTILITY (12:15–21)

Realizing that the Pharisees were plotting against Him, Jesus withdrew from the area of greatest danger.

■ *Jesus' time to die had not yet come. He con-*
■ *tinued His ministry of teaching and healing.*

## THE UNPARDONABLE SIN (12:22–37)

Jesus healed two men, one a mute and the other a blind man. However, the Pharisees made their familiar claim that Jesus' exorcising of demons was really the work of Beelzebub, the prince of demons. Jesus then illustrated the correct interpretation of His exorcisms with a short parable. No one can attack a well-guarded home without first rendering the guard powerless. The point of the parable is that Jesus' exorcisms demonstrate that God through Christ is decisively defeating the devil.

The Unpardonable Sin

The unpardonable sin involves setting one's mind against the Holy Spirit and crediting Satan with what is God's work. To do so is to blaspheme against the Holy Spirit. To "blaspheme" means to speak an insult against someone so as to defame that person's reputation and character.

Jesus then explained to His accusers about the one sin for which there is no forgiveness. Forgiveness is possible for all kinds of sins when a person repents, but blasphemy against the Holy Spirit is the unpardonable sin. He asked His audience of Pharisees to come clean, calling them a "brood of vipers" (v. 34), echoing John the Baptist's words in Matt. 3:7.

■ *The unpardonable sin is not restricted to*
■ *Jesus' day. It happens today when a person*

- *sees a work that is without question God's*
- *work, but claims it is Satan's.*

## THE DEMAND FOR A SIGN (12:38–45)

Some of the scribes and Pharisees asked Jesus to give them a sign to prove His identity. To ask for a sign was an evidence of unbelief, and Jesus viewed their demand as such.

Jesus told them they would receive a sign, but that it would not come on their demand. He used Jonah as an analogy. Just as Jonah's message was God's sign to the Ninevites, and Solomon represented God's wisdom to the Queen of Sheba, Jesus was God's sign to the Jews.

Jesus' sign would be the "sign of the prophet Jonah." Just as Jonah spent three days and nights inside a big fish, Jesus would spend three days and nights in the realm of the dead before coming forth resurrected from death, as Jonah had emerged from the big fish.

- *The unbelief of the Jews caused them to*
- *demand a sign. Jesus offered only the "sign of*
- *Jonah."*

## JESUS' TRUE FAMILY (12:46–50)

Before Jesus was finished speaking with the scribes and Pharisees, His brothers and mother came to Him. Despite the growing rejection of Jesus, His mother and brothers had been wanting to get through the crowd to speak to Him.

After He became aware that His family was present, Jesus pointed to His disciples and said, "Here are my mother and brothers." He was willing to put God's will above the will of His beloved family.

- *Believers as people should care for one*
- *another as if they were family members.*

■ How powerful a witness to the world would
■ be a display of family-like unity in the
■ Church!

## QUESTIONS TO GUIDE YOUR STUDY

1. What was the significance of "Jonah's sign"?
2. What was Jesus' point in referring to His disciples as "my mother and my brothers"?

# MATTHEW 13

This section of Matthew begins the third major block of Jesus' teaching, which is an entire sermon comprised of a series of seven interrelated parables and an added eighth. These parables comprise a dazzling array of stories in which the nature of the kingdom, or the rule of God, is explained.

**Parable**

*Parable* means "a putting alongside for purposes of comparison and new understanding." Parables utilize pictures such as metaphors or similes, and frequently extend them into a brief story to make a point or disclosure.

## THE PARABLE OF THE SOWER (13:1–9)

### The Parable (vv. 1–8)

Jesus told the crowd about a farmer who sowed his field. The sower's seed fell on four different kinds of soil:

1. Some seed fell on the hard pathways in the field. Birds came and ate that seed.
2. Some seed fell on soil thinly covering by a layer of rock. Warmth caused those seeds to germinate quickly. But the sun caused the seeds to wither and die, since they could not take root.
3. Some seed fell on deeper soil that contained thorns. The seeds grew for a while, but the thorns choked them out.

4. Fortunately, some seed fell on good soil. Those seeds grew, and the harvest of grain was abundant.

### The Challenge (v. 9)

 Jesus ended this parable with a challenge to those who heard Him: "He who has ears, let him hear." He was telling the crowd to be like the good soil, letting the seed of the gospel produce an abundant harvest in them.

## JESUS' REASON FOR TEACHING IN PARABLES (13:10–17)

The disciples asked Jesus why He spoke in parables. Although Jesus' answer is difficult to interpret, the reason points to a principle involving human response. He tells them that because of their receptivity, they had been able to understand His parables. The crowds, for the most part, lacked this receptivity. Those who were already receptive would be given increased understanding. Those closed to the truth would become even more blind and deaf to it.

- Of the four kinds of soil in the parable, only
- one is good. Only true believers will bear the
- proper spiritual fruit.

## THE PARABLE OF THE WHEAT AND THE WEEDS (13:24–30)

This parable speaks of two different kinds of seeds sown by two different people, a farmer and his enemy. Weeds (darnel), at first, are often indistinguishable from wheat. Upon discovering weeds among his grain, the patient farmer decides not to risk pulling the weeds before the

**Counterfeits**

Satan employs many counterfeits for the things of God. He uses counterfeit Christians (2 Cor. 11:26) and a counterfeit gospel (Gal. 1:6–9). He encourages a counterfeit righteousness (Rom. 10:1–3), and has a counterfeit church (Rev. 2:9). And, at the end of the age, he will produce a counterfeit Christ (2 Thess. 2:1–12).

harvest, as some of the wheat might be lost in the process. When harvesttime comes, he will have the reapers first gather and then destroy the weeds. Jesus later explains this parable in verses 36–43.

### Summary of the Parable of the Wheat and the Weeds:

 Main Point: God permits the righteous and wicked to coexist in this age, but eventually He will separate the wicked, then judge and destroy them.

■ *Where there are genuine Christians, there*
■ *are also counterfeits. Discovering and com-*
■ *pletely rooting out counterfeits may not be*
■ *possible given our limited knowledge.*

## THE PARABLES OF THE MUSTARD SEED AND THE LEAVEN (13:31–33)

### The Mustard Seed (vv. 31–32)
Jesus told a pair of parables about the growth of God's kingdom. He first compared God's kingdom to what happens when a tiny mustard seed is sown. That little seed grows into a treelike plant as high as ten feet—large enough for birds to nest in its branches.

### The Leaven (v. 33)
He then compared God's kingdom to what happens when a little leaven is added to a batch of meal. Only a small amount of leaven is required to make dough rise. The increase in size brought about by leaven is one of Jesus' points.

- *Small beginnings lead to great results. Like*
- *leaven, the kingdom will be an unseen but*
- *powerful force working within the world to*
- *bring about transformation.*

## THE PARABLES OF THE HIDDEN TREASURES AND THE PEARL OF GREAT PRICE (13:44–45)

### *The Hidden Treasure (v. 44)*

Jesus compared a person who enters the kingdom to a man who sells everything he owns to buy a field containing a treasure that will more than compensate for his sacrifice.

### *The Pearl of Great Price (v. 45)*

Jesus makes the same point by describing a merchant who purchases a costly pearl. Again, the man gives up everything to obtain his treasure.

Jesus was using these parables to call His readers to a choice. He was offering an opportunity for them to live under God's rule.

## THE PARABLE OF THE DRAGNET (13:47–50)

This parable concerns a net used in fishing. Jesus reminds His hearers how a net, when thrown into the water, gathers in all kinds of fish. Then, after returning to the shore, the fishermen separate the good fish from the bad. "Bad" fish were those inedible according to Jewish Law.

This parable points to the mixed character of the Church. At the end of the age, God will separate the righteous from the wicked, sending the wicked ones into the "fiery furnace" (v. 50.)

## THE PARABLE OF THE SCRIBE TRAINED FOR THE KINGDOM (13:51–52)

Jesus compares His disciples to a householder who uses both his old and new possessions and goods to care for the needs of his family and guests. Jesus' disciples will combine their knowledge of God's past revelation in the Old Testament with their growing knowledge of a new, fuller revelation in Jesus.

■ *Only by relating the old to the new could the*
■ *disciples meet the needs of those to whom*
■ *they will minister.*

## JESUS' REJECTION IN HIS OWN HOMETOWN (13:52–58)

"A prophet is honored everywhere except in his hometown and in his own home." (13:57, NCV). This saying is found in Jewish, Greek, and Roman writings.

Jesus briefly returned to His hometown, Nazareth, to teach in the synagogue. It turned out that the people knew Him as the son of Joseph, the carpenter. They were too familiar with Jesus and His family to believe that He was anyone out of the ordinary. Matthew records that the people took offense at Him. Jesus found curiosity, jealousy, and outright hatred in Nazareth; but He found very little faith.

## QUESTIONS TO GUIDE YOUR STUDY

1. Why did Jesus teach in parables?
2. Which of the kingdom parables especially grabs your attention? Why?

## THE DEATH OF JOHN THE BAPTIST (14:1–12)

Herod Antipas, a son of Herod the Great, ruled Galilee at the time. He had imprisoned John because of John's denunciation of his marriage to Herodias. Divorcing his own wife, Herod had married Herodias. John the Baptist had openly criticized the marriage as unlawful and, therefore, adultery.

Jewish Law did not permit a person to be executed without a trial. Neither did it allow beheading as a form of execution. Yet Herod had his hated critic put to death without a trial.

## THE FEEDING OF MORE THAN FIVE THOUSAND (14:13–21)

After hearing of John the Baptist's death, Jesus withdrew to an unpopulated area east of Galilee. The crowds, however, would not leave Jesus alone. Jesus had compassion for them and performed healings. Evening came, and no provision had been made for food. A survey of available food turned up five loaves and two fishes. Using these limited supplies, Jesus miraculously multiplied the food and fed the entire crowd, with twelve full baskets of food left over.

- *The miraculous feeding of the five thousand,*
- *then and now, assures us that whatever our*
- *needs may be, God has more than adequate*
- *resources to meet them.*

**Sea of Galilee**

Also called Lake of Gennesaret. Galilee means circle. A freshwater lake nestled in the hills of northern Palestine. It is thirteen miles long and eight miles wide. In the first century, the Sea of Galilee was of major commercial significance. The fishing industry flourished there.

## MIRACLES ON THE SEA OF GALILEE (14:22–34)

### *The Storm (vv. 22–24)*

After the feeding of the crowd, Jesus made His disciples get into a boat to go to the other side of the Sea of Galilee.

When the crowd and the disciples were gone, Jesus went into the hills by Himself to pray. Meanwhile, the disciples, about halfway across the Sea of Galilee, were battling a storm.

### *Jesus Walks on the Water (vv. 25–27)*

In the midst of the storm, Jesus came walking toward them on the water. At first, the disciples, caught up in their circumstances, thought they were seeing a ghost.

■ *Jesus told them to take courage. It is interest-*
■ *ing to note that Jesus' statement, "It is I," is*
■ *literally "I am." This is a conscious echo of*
■ *the divine name of Yahweh (Exod. 3:14).*

### *Peter Walks on the Water (vv. 28–31)*

**Doubt**

The Greek word translated "doubt" suggests the idea of going two different directions at once.

Upon seeing Jesus walking on the water, Peter asked Jesus to enable him to do the same thing. We do not know Peter's motive for wanting to do so. Jesus agreed and enabled Peter to start walking toward Him. Before he reached Jesus, Peter began to "doubt" his ability to continue. Peter was more focused on the surrounding storm than on the Lord. As a result, Peter began to sink and had to be rescued.

When Jesus and Peter stepped into the boat, the wind stopped blowing. Then the disciples had the assurance they needed. As a result, they worshiped Jesus as the Son of God.

The disciples landed at Gennesaret, where many sick people were brought to Jesus. All who touched even the fringe of His garment were healed.

■ *In the midst of the storm, Jesus went to the*
■ *disciples and saved them. It is interesting to*
■ *note that the very waves that were frighten-*
■ *ing the disciples were the waves that brought*
■ *Jesus to them.*

## QUESTIONS TO GUIDE YOUR STUDY

1. What aspect of the feeding of the five thousand impacted you the most?
2. Describe the circumstances of the storm that threatened the disciples. What encouragement can we gain from this account of Jesus calming the storm?
3. What feelings and thoughts do you believe Peter was experiencing after Jesus rescued him from sinking and as they walked into the boat?

## MATTHEW 15

### CONFLICT WITH THE PHARISEES AND SCRIBES (15:1–20)

A group of Pharisees and scribes came to see Jesus. They were on a fact-finding mission to investigate His activities and teachings. They began by asking Him why His disciples didn't wash their hands before eating.

### A Question about Handwashing (vv. 1–9)

This question had nothing to do with hygiene; it was strictly a matter of ritual. The group accused Jesus of violating rabbinic tradition by eating bread with hands not washed in the proper rabbinic tradition.

### What Defiles a Person (vv. 10–20)

"These people say they love me; they show honor to me with words, but their hearts are far from me."
Isa. 29:13

Jesus answered His accusers by employing a standard rabbinic technique of replying directly with a counterquestion. He used a quote from Isa. 29:13 to describe their behavior.

Jesus taught that a person is not defiled by what he puts into his mouth. The primary source of evil is internal, from the evil of the human heart.

Jesus called the Pharisees "blind guides" (v. 13), because they failed to see the truth of His identity and teaching. The equally blind people they led would fall with them.

■ *Moral purity and the keeping of God's Word*
■ *begins within a person's heart—one's*
■ *thoughts and will.*

## A CANAANITE WOMAN'S FAITH (15:21–28)

This woman was a Gentile. "Canaanite" was a general term for the pagan inhabitants of the Promised Land which Israel was told to conquer in Joshua's day. She pleaded for Jesus to heal her demon-possessed daughter. She was persistent in her plea, and she had a tenacious faith. Jesus marveled at her faith. It was in stark contrast to the lack of faith exhibited by the religious leaders. Jesus responded to this woman's faith and granted her request. From a distance, He healed her daughter immediately.

## THE FEEDING OF MORE THAN FOUR THOUSAND (15:29–39)

This feeding contains too many differences to be a variant account of the same incident.

As before, Jesus asked about the available resources. This time there were seven loaves and some small fish. Taking, blessing, and breaking the food, Jesus gave it to the disciples for distribution to the crowd. After all the people had been fed, seven baskets of food remained.

- This second feeding miracle emphasized the fact
- that although His primary mission was to Jews,
- Jesus could act on behalf of the Gentiles as well.

## QUESTIONS TO GUIDE YOUR STUDY

1. Jesus taught that the primary source of defilement came from the heart. What examples of "heart defilement" might believers want to avoid?
2. What about the Canaanite woman's faith impressed Jesus?

# MATTHEW 16

## A DEMAND FROM THE RELIGIOUS AUTHORITIES FOR A SIGN (16:1–12)

The Pharisees and Sadducees demanded a sign from Jesus that proved the divine origin of Jesus' exorcisms. Their purpose was to test Him and possibly diminish His influence with the people.

**"On this rock"**

This phrase denotes a ledge or cliff or rock like that referred to in Matthew 7:24 on which the wise man built his house. *Petros*, the Greek word for Peter, refers to a smaller detachment of a massive ledge. But A.T. Robertson says, ". . . Too much must not be made of this point since Jesus probably spoke Aramaic to Peter which draws no such distinction." WPNT, I p. 131

## SIMON PETER'S RECOGNITION OF JESUS' IDENTITY (16:13–20)

Jesus posed a question to the disciples: "Who do people say the Son of Man is?" (v. 13). The disciples responded with several opinions. Peter acted as spokesman for the group, saying, "You are the Christ, the Son of the living God" (v. 16). This is the first time in Matthew that anyone in Jesus' audience has acknowledged Him as the "Christ."

Jesus praised Simon for his confession of faith. He declared that this insight had come from God, not from human sources. He gave Simon a new name—Peter, which means "rock." The rock on which the Church is built is the faith shown by Peter in making his confession.

■ *The recognition of Jesus' messiahship*
■ *marked an important step in the disciples'*
■ *understanding of Jesus. However, He was not*
■ *to be the kind of Messiah the Jews expected.*

## THE PATH OF CHRIST AND HIS FOLLOWERS (16:21–28)

Building on Peter's confession, Jesus began to teach His disciples what His messiahship actually involved. He would be a suffering messiah, not a military warrior or a political leader. The disciples would follow Jesus along the same path, many becoming martyrs for their faith.

■ *Following Christ is a life of self-denial. It*
■ *means to give oneself wholly to Christ and to*
■ *share in His rejection, shame, suffering, and*

■ *death. As with Jesus, His followers' suffering*
■ *will lead to glory.*

## QUESTIONS TO GUIDE YOUR STUDY

1. The Jewish authorities demanded a sign from Jesus. What might have been their proper approach to Jesus?
2. To follow Christ is a commitment to self-denial. What does self-denial involve?
3. What was the disciples' understanding of Jesus' messiahship at this point in Matthew's narrative?

## MATTHEW 17

### THE TRANSFIGURATION (17:1–13)

Jesus took the three inner-circle disciples—Peter, James, and John—with Him up on a high mountain. Some have suggested Mount Tabor; others, Mount Hermon. There the disciples saw Jesus transfigured before their eyes. For that brief moment, they saw Jesus as the heavenly Lord. His personal appearance and that of His garments were changed. His skin and clothes shone with dazzling brilliance and whiteness, suggesting glory, sovereignty, and purity. This event was a foreshadowing of Jesus' future glory.

As the disciples watched, Moses and Elijah appeared and spoke with Jesus.

Evidently Peter, not understanding what was happening, wanted to prolong the vision. He began to speak about setting up shelters for Jesus, Moses, and Elijah so they could stay

In this picture, Moses symbolized the Law, while Elijah stood for the Prophets. Jesus had come to fulfill both. Both Moses and Elijah were connected in Old Testament writings with the age of the Messiah. Their appearance with Jesus meant in part that He was the prophet whom Moses foretold in Deut. 18:15 and the Messiah whom Elijah would precede, as foreseen in Mal. 4:5.

**Transfiguration**

The word *transfigured*, in more common English, is translated "transformed." The Greek word used is *metamorphoo*, from which we get the English word *metamorphosis*.

longer. Then a bright cloud overshadowed them. The voice of God spoke from the cloud and said, "This is my Son, whom I love: with him I am well pleased. Listen to him!" (v. 5).

The awestruck disciples "fell facedown to the ground" (v. 6). Based on the Greek word Matthew used, the disciples' fear was more terror than reverence, although their posture may have suggested an element of worship.

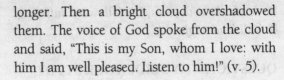

■ *The transfiguration was a foreshadowing of*
■ *Jesus' resurrection and return.*

## THE DISCIPLES' LACK OF FAITH (17:14–21)

The overwhelming experience on the mountain soon gave way to everyday reality. Jesus and the three disciples returned from the mountain. While they were away, a crowd had gathered with the nine remaining disciples. During Jesus' absence, the nine disciples had tried to heal an epileptic boy, but without success.

**"Little Faith"**

One of Matthew's favorite adjectives is a word translated "little faith." Matthew uses it five times in his Gospel (6:30; 8:26; 14:31; 16:8; 17:20). The word is really a combination of two words: meaning "a small amount" and "faith." Jesus spoke this word as a tender rebuke during the disciples' times of anxiety.

The disciples asked Jesus why they had not been able to heal the boy. (After all, He had given them the authority to heal the sick.) Jesus blamed their failure on their lack of faith, or better, minuscule faith.

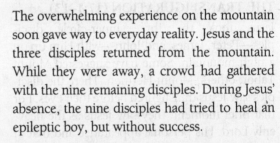

■ *It is important to cultivate faith. Faith "as*
■ *small as a mustard seed" suggests not only*
■ *little faith, but also life and growth.*

## MORE WORDS FORETELLING JESUS' DEATH (17:22–23)

In these two verses Jesus tried to prepare the disciples for what to expect on their coming visit to Jerusalem. He explained that He would be arrested and killed. Yet He would be raised on the third day after His death. The disciples were "filled with grief" (v. 23). Although they were becoming accustomed to the fact of Jesus' coming death, they were finding the idea very troublesome.

## A QUESTION ABOUT TAXES (17:24–27)

Poll-tax collectors came to Peter and asked him whether Jesus paid the annual half-shekel tax which Jewish males were required to pay for temple upkeep.

Jesus took the opportunity to teach an important lesson. As sons of the kingdom, He and His disciples should be exempt from having to pay the temple tax. So as not to offend the Jews He was trying to reach, however, He would pay the tax. He then gave instructions to Peter to catch a fish. The first fish he would catch would have a shekel in its mouth. With that shekel, Peter was to pay the tax for himself and Jesus.

■ *If Jesus and His followers had failed to pay*
■ *this religious tax, most likely others would*
■ *have misunderstood. The loving thing for*
■ *Jesus and His disciples to do was to take into*
■ *account their influence on others and pay the*
■ *tax. Concern for others is a valid reason for*
■ *not always exercising one's rights.*

From Luke's account, we know their conversation with Jesus concerned His coming death.

Taxes in Jesus' Day

In the New Testament era, Herod the Great levied a tax on the produce of the field and a tax on items bought and sold. Other duties paid to foreign powers were:

• a land tax
• a poll tax
• a kind of progressive income tax;
• a personal property tax and
• a house tax levied in Jerusalem.

Taxes were paid directly to Roman authorities. The Israelites resented most deeply the duties paid to the occupying powers. Many zealous Jews considered it treason to God to pay taxes to Rome. When questioned about paying the poll tax, Jesus surprised His questioners by saying that the law should be obeyed.

## QUESTIONS TO GUIDE YOUR STUDY

1. What was the significance of the Transfiguration?

2. What steps might we take to resolve "little faith"?

3. Considering Jesus' other miracles, what is different about His healing of the boy with a demon?

# MATTHEW 18 . . . . . . . . . . . . . . . .

## GREATNESS IN THE KINGDOM (18:1–4)

### The Disciple's Question (v. 1)

The disciples came to Jesus with a question. "Who is the greatest in the kingdom of heaven?"

The asking of the question, however, revealed a serious misunderstanding on their part about the nature of God's kingdom. And, in light of Jesus' recent and repeated predictions of His own death and teaching on self-denial, the question seemed highly inappropriate.

### How to Enter the Kingdom (vv. 2–3)

Jesus called a child to Himself and told the disciples they must "change and become like little children" (v. 2), or they would never enter God's kingdom.

### The Greatest in the Kingdom (v. 4)

The greatest person in the kingdom is one who "humbles himself like this child" (v. 4). This is a question every follower of Jesus should ask regularly in retrospect: Is my confidence like that of a child who trusts the goodness of the Father, or is my confidence in myself?

In his Gospel, Mark tells us that the disciples had been discussing this question among themselves. Luke tells us they even reached the point of arguing about it (Luke 9:46).

- *Too often we concern ourselves with our sta-*
- *tus here and now. Jesus represented a rever-*
- *sal of the world's values. He counted humility*
- *as the mark of greatness.*

## RESPONSIBILITIES TOWARD LITTLE ONES (18:5–6)

Jesus identified Himself with children and the lowly people whom the world ignored or rejected. To receive a child or a child in faith (a new or immature Christian) in Jesus' name, as His representative, is to receive Jesus Himself.

Jesus emphasized the seriousness of causing a weaker Christian to sin. Better to have a large millstone hung around one's neck and be cast into the sea than to cause a little one to sin.

- *As representatives of Jesus Christ, we need to*
- *be examples to others in the faith.*

## WHAT TO DO ABOUT TEMPTATION (18:7–9)

Jesus goes on to teach His disciples more about the problem of temptations. He makes an important point that we must be careful not to be the means by which temptations come to others. We need to exercise the kind of self-discipline that will rid our lives of whatever is causing a temptation to sin.

Temptation

The Greek word is *skandalon* which can also mean stumbling block, hindrance, trap, snare, or something that causes us to fall.

- *Faithful dependence on God, regardless of how*
- *others treat us, makes us great in God's eyes.*

## THE LOST SHEEP (18:10–14)

Jesus stressed the untold value God places on every person, irregardless of that person's status by earthly standards. To illustrate this, Jesus told a parable about a lost sheep. Jesus declares that the shepherd will not be content until all the sheep are safe. He will leave the flock to look for that lost sheep until he finds it.

■ *We should humble ourselves and never cause*
■ *others to sin. God never despises His people,*
■ *but is always concerned to go to great lengths*
■ *to preserve them. God does all He can to*
■ *make certain that none of them will perish.*

## DISCIPLINE WITHIN THE CHURCH (18:15–17)

In His Sermon on the Mount, Jesus taught the necessity for making things right with a brother whom one had offended before bringing an offering to God. He placed responsibility on the wrongdoer for bringing about reconciliation. In this passage, Jesus describes a four-step procedure for dealing with the problem of being wronged by a brother. Those steps are outlined on the following page.

■ *Discipline within the church is necessary to*
■ *avoid compromising the unity and testimony*
■ *of God's people. Jesus taught that complaints*
■ *between believers must be reconciled and*
■ *relationships restored.*

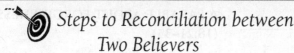

## Steps to Reconciliation between Two Believers

1. Confront the fellow believer. Ideally, the two should resolve the problem without involving anyone else.

2. If the first step fails, the offended believer is to take two or three other believers with him. The other believers can observe the attitudes and motives of the two and attempt to bring reconciliation.

3. If step two fails, the matter should be brought before the assembled church. Here, restoration and reconciliation are to be the goals.

4. If the church fails to bring harmony, the church is to exclude the erring believer from the fellowship because of his or her unwillingness to overcome the barrier with the offended believer.

## THE AUTHORITY OF THE CHURCH (18:18–20)

Earlier, Jesus had promised Peter the authority to "bind" and "loose" (cf. 16:19). Here the church's authority seems to apply also to the right to accept or expel members. The church's loosing and binding—forgiving or refusing to forgive—carries the authority of God. The church's actions, however, are to conform to Jesus' teaching and not be arbitrary. The church has the responsibility of obtaining God's guidance in decision making.

God promised to be with any two or three believers who come together to pray in His name. God, of course, is omnipresent, but He is uniquely present in every Christian gathering as His Spirit indwells believers.

"Where There are Two or Three"

"For where there are two or three who have been joined together into my Name with the result that I am the common object of their faith, there I am in their midst."
Kenneth S. Wuest, *The New Testament: An Expanded Translation*, p. 47.

- The Jews believed that God's divine presence
- was with those engaged in studying the Law.
- Jesus promised to be that divine presence in
- the midst of those gathered to seek His will.

## A PARABLE ABOUT FORGIVENESS (18:21–35)

Here is the fifth and last of the uniquely Matthean accounts involving Peter.

### A Question and an Answer (vv. 21–22)

Peter, probably acting as spokesman for the group, asked Jesus how often it was necessary to forgive a fellow believer. He generously proposed seven times, which went beyond the rabbinic maxim for forgiving three times. But Jesus tells Peter he should be ready to forgive seventy-seven times!

### A Parable (vv. 23–34)

Jesus told a parable found only here in Matthew's Gospel. The parable teaches the importance of forgiveness. A king decided to "settle accounts" with his servants. One of the servants owed the king ten thousand talents (estimates range from several million to one trillion dollars), but he had no way of repaying the debt. The king ordered the debtor and his family sold, along with all his possessions.

Falling to his knees, the indebted servant promised to repay all he owed if the king would not carry out the intended punishment. The king took pity on the servant and canceled his enormous debt.

But as the servant was leaving the king's presence, he met a fellow servant who owed him a small sum. You might expect the servant to forgive gladly the small debt since he had just had his enormous debt canceled by the king. Instead, the servant grabbed the man by the throat and demanded payment, refusing to listen to the man's pleas for mercy, and threw him into prison.

Upon hearing what the servant had done, the king ordered him imprisoned until he could pay the debt.

### The Parable's Application (v. 35)

Jesus applied this parable to the lives of His hearers. No forgiveness we might show can compare to the forgiveness already shown us by God. If we are not willing to forgive a fellow believer from the heart, we will find no forgiveness from God. An unforgiving person is incapable of receiving God's forgiveness.

1. God takes the initiative to go to great lengths to bring to Him those who have strayed.
2. Reclaiming such people should lead to joyous celebration.
3. The faithfulness of the majority should never excuse us for ignoring anyone who remains distant from God.

**N**

■ *Three themes emerge from this parable:*
■ *(1) God's boundless grace, (2) the absurdity*
■ *of spurning that grace, and (3) the frightful*
■ *fate awaiting the unforgiving.*

## QUESTIONS TO GUIDE YOUR STUDY

1. What should be our attitude toward a new or weaker believer in the faith?
2. Jesus spoke strongly about the problem of temptation. What preventive steps might we take to prepare for times when temptations come?
3. Describe Jesus' qualities as Shepherd. In what ways have you benefited from His shepherding in your life?

In Jesus' day, the rabbinic school of Hillel held that divorce was lawful for almost any cause. According to this school, a man was justified in divorcing his wife for burning his dinner! The school of Shammai, in contrast, held that only the wife's adultery was a lawful reason for divorce. The wording of the text reflects only a man's perspective, since women were rarely, if ever, able to divorce in ancient Judaism.

From early times provision was made for divorce among the Israelites (Deut. 24:1–4). Presumably prior to this decree, a wife could be put out of the home at the pleasure of her husband. Now he was required to write out "a bill of divorce" and give it to his wife as proof he was divorcing her. This gave some dignity and protection to the divorced woman.

# MATTHEW 19 . . . . . . . . . . . . . . . . . . .

## TEACHINGS ABOUT DIVORCE (19:1–12)

### The Question (v. 3)

This time the Pharisees asked Jesus a question about divorce to test Him. They asked whether it was lawful for a man to divorce his wife for any reason.

### Back to the Beginning (v. 4)

Jesus quoted from Genesis and pointed out that the marriage covenant has two parts: "leave . . . and be united." That means "to transfer one's fundamental allegiance from parents to spouse."

### The Pharisees' Counterquestion (vv. 7–9)

The Pharisees countered with a question about Moses' statement that a man could divorce his wife by giving her "a certificate of divorce." The Pharisees' counterquestion raised the obvious objection: Why did God permit divorce in Old Testament times if He categorically opposed it?

In His reply, Jesus went beyond both competing schools of Pharisaic thought—the Hillelites, who granted divorce "for any good cause," and the Shammaites, who limited it to adultery. Jesus emphasized the permanence of marriage as God's original design.

### The Disciples' Reaction and Jesus' Reply (vv. 10–12)

The disciples were amazed at Jesus' teaching. They declared that it might be better for a man not to marry at all if God's ideal for marriage was so high.

■ *God's provision for divorce was temporary,*
■ *based on the rebellion of fallen humanity.*

## BLESSING THE CHILDREN (19:13–15)

In this section Jesus dealt with His disciples' impatience at certain individuals who asked Him to bless their children. Jesus overruled His disciples and invited the children to come to Him.

## DEMANDS OF THE KINGDOM (19:16–26)

### The Young Man's Question (v. 16–22)

A man came to Jesus and wanted to know what he must do to gain eternal life. Jesus was not satisfied with the young man's obvious Jewish answer to His question. The man wanted to limit what he had to do. Jesus diverted the young man's attention from his inadequate criteria of entering into life and focusing on the standard of divine goodness.

■ *Three lessons from this event touch all of us:*
■ *1. One can be interested in eternal life with*
■ *out possessing it (v. 17).*
■ *2. Many who claim to have obeyed God have*
■ *done so only in a superficial way (v. 20).*
■ *3. The young man lacked eternal life because*
■ *he rejected Jesus' call for repentance (v. 22).*

### The Danger in Riches (vv. 23–26)

Jesus now begins a dialogue, with His disciples. He says it's easier for a camel to pass through the eye of a needle than for a rich man to enter the kingdom of God.

A Psychological Paradox

The young man claims to have kept all these commandments and yet he was not satisfied. He had an uneasy conscience and Jesus called him to something he did not have.
A.T. Robertson, *WPNT*, I., p. 157.

"Needle"

Matthew uses the word for an ordinary needle, whereas Luke (18:25) uses the term for a surgical needle.

Many who are first will be last, and many who are last will be first. Many who had apparently accomplished much and so seemed to deserve much will be surprised to find themselves last in the kingdom. Many who had assumed they would be last will, in reality, be first.

## THE REWARDS FOR CHRIST'S DISCIPLES (19:27–30)

In contrast to the young man who would not sacrifice his wealth to follow Jesus, the disciples had given up a great deal of earthly security to follow Him. Peter reminded Jesus of this and asked Him what kind of reward they might receive. Jesus assured them that in the world to come, they would receive a hundred times what they sacrificed, together with eternal life.

- In God's kingdom, earthly values will be
- reversed. The "hundred-fold" compensation
- Jesus promised His followers will be more won-
- derful than anything this earth has to offer.

## QUESTIONS TO GUIDE YOUR STUDY

1. How did Jesus answer the Pharisees' question about divorce?
2. Why did Jesus have a special concern for children?
3. What prevented the young man from following Jesus?

# MATTHEW 20

## THE PARABLE OF THE VINEYARD WORKERS (20:1–16)

Jesus pictured harvesttime, during which a farmer hired a certain number of seasonal workers each day according to his needs. He went to the marketplace, the center of town, at about six o'clock in the morning and hired a group of laborers for one day's work. At about nine o'clock, seeing others who needed work standing in the marketplace, he hired yet another group. Then, at about noon and at three o'clock he hired more laborers. Finally at five o'clock, with only an hour left in the workday, he hired a few more workers.

At six o'clock in the evening, the farmer instructed his steward to pay the workers, beginning with those hired last and ending with those he hired first (at six o'clock in the morning).

Surprisingly, those who had worked only one hour received a full day's pay, just as those who had worked long and hard for twelve hours. Those who had worked all day complained to the farmer. They couldn't deny that he had kept his part of the bargain, as he had paid them what he promised. They were jealous of those who had been paid as much as they after so little work, and they became angry because they hadn't received a bonus.

 Main point: God's grace does not contradict standards of fairness, but exeeds them.

■ *This parable emphasizes a right attitude in*
■ *service. God is generous and will always give*
■ *us better than we deserve.*

## JESUS' THIRD STATEMENT ABOUT HIS DEATH (20:17–19)

On the way to Jerusalem, Jesus again tells His disciples what will happen there. He will be delivered to His enemies, the scribes and chief priests. These religious leader will condemn Him. They will then deliver Him to the Romans

Twice before He had tried to explain these coming events to them, but they had not understood (16:21–23; 17:22–23). Now Jesus tells them what will happen in greater detail than before.

(Gentiles) for mockery, scourging, and execution by crucifixion. But, on the third day, He will be raised from death.

■ *The exalted Son of God must first become*
■ *God's Suffering Servant and die. Few,*
■ *including the twelve disciples, are ready for*
■ *this.*

## MORE ABOUT GREATNESS (20:20–28)

The mother of James and John came with them to make a special request of Jesus. Kneeling before Him, she asked that her two sons be given special places of honor in His kingdom, one at His right hand, one at His left. It is almost certain that James and John had their mother make this request for them.

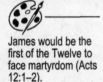

James would be the first of the Twelve to face martyrdom (Acts 12:1–2).

Jesus explained to these two close disciples that they didn't really know what they were asking. He had been talking about His coming death, while they were thinking about their "proper place" in the kingdom. He then redirected their attention to His coming suffering. His question, "Can you drink the cup I am going to drink?" (v. 22) was really asking if they were ready to die with Him.

Jesus assured them that they *would* drink His cup.

Verse 28 stands among the most valuable in Matthew's Gospel. In it Jesus declares that He has come to serve rather than to be served. He has come to give His life as a ransom for many.

The word *many* (v. 28) refers to all who accept Jesus' offer of forgiveness, made possible by His death, and who commit their lives to Him in discipleship.

- *Jesus declared that the decision as to who*
- *would have positions of honor in His king-*
- *dom was not His to make. Only the Father*
- *Himself knew who would occupy the places*
- *of honor.*

## THE HEALING OF THE TWO BLIND MEN (20:29–34)

Jesus and His disciples left Jericho, followed by a large crowd. As they traveled, they came upon two blind men sitting beside the crowd. Hearing that Jesus was passing that way, the two men cried out to Him for mercy, using the messianic title "Son of David" (v. 30). The crowd tried to quiet the men. Perhaps the crowd feared trouble from the authorities if Jesus were publicly called the Messiah.

But Jesus heard the repeated cries of the blind men and asked what they wanted. At their request, out of compassion, He healed them both. The men were so grateful for their healing that they became Jesus' followers.

## QUESTIONS TO GUIDE YOUR STUDY

1. Why were the vineyard farmer's payments for labor fair to all the workers?
2. What is the lesson of the parable of the vineyard?
3. Why was it so difficult for the disciples to accept a Suffering Servant as the Messiah?

"Ransom"

This word is one commonly employed as the price for a slave who is then set free by the one who bought him. Jesus gave His own life as the price of freedom for the slaves of sin.
A.T. Robertson, *WPNT* I, p. 163

Jericho

In Jesus' day Jericho was a prominent city of Judea, strategically located on the route from Galilee to Jerusalem. It was the last major city one passed through before climbing the treacherous road to Jerusalem. Because it was a wealthy city, it attracted beggars.

"Rejoice greatly, people of Jerusalem! Shout for joy, people of Jerusalem! Your king is coming to you. He does what is right, and he saves. He is gentle and riding on a donkey, on the colt of a donkey."
(Zech. 9:9, NCV)

## ROYAL ENTRY INTO JERUSALEM (21:1–11)

Jesus was nearing Jerusalem and the last days of His earthly life. He planned to make a dramatic entry into the city to make Himself known as the Messiah, but not the kind of Messiah the people were expecting.

The significance of this event for the New Testament writers is obvious since all four Gospels record it. It was Passover, and one estimate has about two and one-half million people present in Jerusalem for the celebration. Jesus could have chosen no better time for symbolically presenting Himself to His people. Yet He was fully aware that the minds of the religious leaders were already set against Him. He could expect nothing but hostility from them. Because of the prevailing circumstances, this account is often misnamed the "triumphal entry."

### Preparation for the Entry (vv. 1–7)

It seems that Jesus had already made plans for a donkey and its colt to be ready for Him. Matthew makes it a point to mention that the colt had never been ridden.

### The Crowd's Response (vv. 8–11)

Although He was riding a donkey, the crowd gave Jesus the kind of greeting they would have given a king. Most laid garments down in His path. Others spread tree branches along the roadside.

The crowds shouted words to Jesus from Ps. 118:26. This is one of the hallel psalms used to greet pilgrims who came to Jerusalem at feast times.

"Bless the one who comes in the name of the Lord. We bless you from the house of the Lord."
(Ps. 118:26, NLT

■ *As Jesus entered Jerusalem, He received a*
■ *king's welcome. The procession had a power-*
■ *ful impact on the inhabitants of the city.*
■ *Added to the cries of "Hosanna" was the title,*
■ *"Son of David."*

## JESUS CLEARS OUT THE TEMPLE (21:12–17)

All four Gospels include the incident of Jesus' cleansing the temple. He found it busy with the activity of money changers and sellers of sacrificial birds and animals. Since sacrificial birds and animals had to be officially certified and unblemished, it was helpful to purchase them at the temple. Evidently, the selling and money changing had become a means of cheating and exploiting the people. Jesus became angry at what He saw. He drove out the merchants and overturned their tables. Instead of attacking the political base of Roman rule, as most would have hoped, Jesus' attack threatened the center of Judaism itself.

■ *Jesus' cleansing the temple of the money-*
■ *changers fulfilled Old Testament prophecy.*

## THE FRUITLESS FIG TREE (21:18–22)

On the following morning, as He returned to Jerusalem from Bethany, Jesus was hungry. He saw a fig tree by the road and thought He would eat some figs from it. Upon closer inspection, however, He found that the tree had only leaves and no fruit.

The rationale for Jesus' behavior is in fact scriptural. As He cleared the area of the various commercial transactions, Jesus began to fulfill the prophecy that a day would come when no "merchant" would remain in the house of God (Zech. 14:21). Jesus then quoted portions of Isa. 56:7 and Jer. 7:11. God's house was to be a house of prayer.

Fig Tree

The common fig tree has a short stout trunk and thick branches and twigs bearing coarsely lobed rough leaves. Rounded fruits ripen during the summer. Figs dry well and were stored as cakes for future use.

Seeing the tree was barren, Jesus declared that the tree would never again bear fruit. The tree immediately withered. Why would Jesus work this destructive miracle? He used the fig tree and its destruction to symbolize Israel's coming fate. To all outward appearances, Israel was full of the promise of spiritual fruit. In reality, Israel was fruitless. Like the fig tree, it would be destroyed because of its barrenness.

■ *Amazing resources are available through the*
■ *prayer of faith. Fruitlessness does not have to*
■ *be the fate of any individual or nation. Faith*
■ *and faith's expression in prayer make it pos-*
■ *sible to bear fruit for God.*

## A QUESTION ABOUT AUTHORITY (21:23–27)

### The Question (v. 23)

The day after the temple cleansing, Jesus went back and began teaching. As He taught, the chief priests and elders came to question Him about His authority.

The chief priests were Sadducees. The elders were scribes or Pharisees, the laymen. Together they made up the membership of the Sanhedrin, the Jewish high council.

### Jesus' Reply (vv. 24–25a)

Jesus agreed to answer the authorities' questions on the condition that they first answer one for Him. He wanted them to tell Him the source of authority for the baptism of John the Baptist. Had it come from God or not?

### The Authorities' Dilemma (vv. 25b–27)

Jesus' reply clearly created a dilemma for the chief priests and elders. To admit that John's authority came from God would be to condemn themselves. John had preached an even more rigorous morality than their own. Jesus would indict them for their lack of belief in John. If they claimed John's source of authority was a merely human one, they would anger the people. The people believed John was a prophet, a messenger from God.

It was a no-win scenario for the authorities. Neither answer was a safe one. The authorities decided to claim ignorance: "We don't know." Because the leaders did not answer His question, Jesus insisted that He would not answer theirs.

■ *In a scheme to trap Jesus, the temple author-*
■ *ities trapped themselves, and could only*
■ *answer Him with a lame expression of igno-*
■ *rance. Since they could not judge John, they*
■ *could not fairly judge Jesus.*

After Jesus refused to answer the leaders' question about His source of authority, He told three parables: the two sons, the wicked tenants, and the marriage feast of the king's son. All three parables were directed against the Jewish leaders, echoing the spiritual failure of official Israel.

## JESUS' PARABLE ABOUT TWO SONS (21:28–32)

In the parable of the two sons, a man told one of his sons to work in his vineyard, but one son refused his father's request. Later that day, however, the son was sorry that he had refused and did go to work The other son said he would go to work, but he did not go.

The son who refused and later changed his mind represented the irreligious Jews, such as publicans and sinners, who were flocking to

**"Regretted"**

Literally means "to be sorry afterwards." A.T. Robertson says, "Here the boy got sorry for his stubborn refusal to obey his father and went and obeyed. Godly sorrow leads to repentance, but mere sorrow is not repentance."
A.T. Robertson
*WPNT* I, p. 170.

Jesus. The son who said, "I will, sir" (v. 30), and did not go to work represented the Jewish religious leaders who failed to recognize God's saving actions in the ministry of Jesus. Jesus commended the irreligious Jews who were repenting, but gave a firm rebuke to the self-righteous Jewish leaders.

■ *Like the second son in the parable, the Jewish*
■ *authorities had promised they would do*
■ *God's will. Yet, they did not believe John the*
■ *Baptist, who had brought them God's*
■ *demand for repentance. God demands real*
■ *obedience, not simply lip service.*

## JESUS' PARABLE ABOUT A VINEYARD'S TENANTS (21:33–41)

### The Story (vv. 33–39)

A man planted a vineyard, equipping it with a hedge for protection from animals, a watch tower, and a winepress. Then he went abroad and left the vineyard in charge of tenants who agreed to pay their rent in the form of part of the yearly crop. When the time came for the grapes to be ready, the owner sent some of his servants to get his share. Instead of giving the servants the fruit, however, the tenants attacked them. One was beaten, one was stoned, and one was murdered. A second group of servants sent by the owner received the same treatment. Finally, the owner sent his son to get the fruit, thinking the tenants would surely respect him. But the servants did not respect the son, and killed him instead.

## A Question and Answer (vv. 40–41)

After delivering the parable, Jesus asked a question of the authorities. His question was, "When the owner of the vineyard comes, what will he do to those tenants?" (v.40). They answered by saying that the owner would naturally put them to death. Then he would give management of the vineyard to new tenants who would give him the fruit he was due. As before, the authorities had condemned themselves with their own words.

## *The Parable's Symbolism*

In this parable, the owner represents God, and the vineyard represents the Jewish nation (Isa. 5:1–7). The tenants who rented the vineyard are the Jewish leaders, and the servants beaten and killed refer to the Old Testament prophets. The son who was murdered represents Jesus. The destruction of the husbandman points to the utter overthrow of the Jewish religious leaders in Jerusalem in A.D. 70. Giving the vineyard to others suggests the transfer of God's kingdom to "God's own people," who would be redeemed Jews and Gentiles (1 Pet. 2:9). Just as the owner expected fruit from the husbandman, God expected fruit from the nation of Israel. Their fruitlessness led to judgment.

## THE CORNERSTONE (21:42–43)

Jesus quoted from Ps. 118:22–23 to warn the leaders about the consequences of rejecting Him. That passage had spoken of a stone rejected by builders but finally made "the head of the corner."

Cornerstone

The stone laid at the corner to bind two walls together and to strengthen them. Used as a symbol of strength and prominence.

- *The kingdom would be taken from the leaders who had not been faithful to God's will.*

## QUESTIONS TO GUIDE YOUR STUDY

1. When Jesus rode into Jerusalem on a donkey, how were the people receiving Him? What were they anticipating?
2. Jesus cleared the temple of the money changers. What drove Him to take such decisive and strong measures?
3. What is the lesson of the fruitless fig tree?

## MATTHEW 22

### INVITATIONS TO A WEDDING BANQUET (22:1–14)

**Banquet**

An elaborate meal, sometimes called a feast, are prominent in sealing friendships and celebrating victories. This latter purpose is seen in Jesus' reference to the messianic banquet.

#### Refusals (vv. 1–7)

Jesus told a story about a king who was planning a wedding banquet for his son. In accordance with oriental custom, the king first sent out servants to give a general invitation to those he wanted to invite. Those who were invited refused the invitations.

When the banquet was prepared, the king again sent out invitations to the same guests, giving them another chance. This time the message declared that the banquet was ready. Most of those invited made excuses for not going. And, incredibly, the rest killed the servants who brought them the invitation. To refuse an invitation was to reject the king's authority. To kill the king's servant was an offense requiring severe punishment. The angry king sent troops to destroy and burn their city.

### The Banquet Guests (vv. 8–10)

Determined to fill the hall for his son's wedding feast, the king sent his servants to bring in all kinds of people, good and bad, from the streets. These became the king's banquet guests.

In this story, Jesus was speaking about the Jewish leaders. They should have been overjoyed to receive an invitation to God's banquet table. Yet, they were hostile or indifferent to the invitation when it came through Jesus. For that reason, God opened the doors of His kingdom to all kinds of people. That is why Jesus' ministry extended to "sinners" and outcasts.

### The Guest without a Wedding Garment (vv. 11–14)

One member of the group appeared without the proper wedding clothes. When questioned why he was not dressed for the occasion, the man offered no excuse. The king had him bound and thrown outside the lighted banquet hall into the darkness. There he could regret what he had done. Jesus concluded the parable by saying, "Many are invited, but few are chosen."

- *God, in His grace, has called many people to*
- *receive His salvation. But those who accept*
- *God's salvation must accept it on His terms.*

## IS IT RIGHT TO PAY TAXES? (22:15–22)

### The Controversial Question (vv. 16–18)

Evidently the three parables Jesus had just delivered enraged the religious authorities, for

Matthew tells us that they met to decide how to best trap Jesus. They decided to do so with a political question: "Is it right to pay taxes to Caesar or not?"

### Jesus' Answer (vv. 19–22)

They had chosen a highly controversial question. Whatever Jesus' answer, He was certain to displease some of the people. Jesus at once saw through the ruse. Calling His questioners hypocrites, He asked for one of the coins with which the tax was to be paid. He then asked them whose image was on the coin, and they answered, "Caesar's."

When Jesus told them, "Give to Caesar what is Caesar's, and to God what is God's" (v. 21), they marveled at His answer, and had no argument.

■ *The emperor had the responsibility for mint-*
■ *ing and circulating the coins bearing his*
■ *image. So the coins actually belonged to him.*
■ *If he requested their return in the form of*
■ *taxes, the people should give back what*
■ *belonged to him. But they must also give back*
■ *to God what belongs to God. Each person*
■ *bears God's image, and God wants each per-*
■ *son given back to Him in total allegiance.*

## THE SADDUCEES' QUESTION (22:23–33)

### The Question (vv. 23–28)

The Sadducees took the stage next. They ridiculed the notion of resurrection by means of a worst-case scenario. They used a deliberately exaggerated example, hoping that Jesus would discredit Himself before the people. Their ques-

**Sadducees**

Small in number, they were a wealthy, aristocratic, and priestly party. This Jewish sect refused to believe in any doctrine that could not be established from the Law, the five books of Moses. Consequently, they did not believe in resurrection from the dead, angels, or oral tradition.

tion was based on Moses' teaching in Deut. 25:4–6.

Moses taught that if brothers lived together, and one died childless, his brother should marry the widow to provide an heir for the dead brother. Suppose, they asked Jesus, seven brothers in turn married the woman, each dying without leaving a child. After his own death, whose wife would the woman be in the resurrection?

### Jesus' Answer (vv. 29–32)
Jesus declared the Sadducees were doubly wrong. First, they assumed any future life would have to be a continuation of this present material life. They did not realize God's power to create a whole new order in the life to come. Second, Jesus told them their denial of the resurrection proved they did not even understand the Scriptures. He then quoted from Exod. 3:6, part of the Scripture they accepted and claimed to understand.

"I am the God of your ancestors—the God of Abraham, the God of Isaac, and the God of Jacob."
(Exod. 3:6, NCV)

### The People's Reaction (v. 33)
Jesus' response was unanswerable. In spite of the Sadducees' attempt to hurt Jesus, the crowds "were astonished at his teaching."

■ *Answers to questions about the future must*
■ *rest on the authority of God's Word. The Sad-*
■ *ducees were not only foolish, but ignorant of*
■ *the Old Testament Scriptures. Jesus had so*
■ *completely answered them that they were*
■ *"silenced."*

## THE TWO GREATEST COMMANDMENTS (22:34–40)
To this point, the Pharisees had sent their disciples and others to trap Jesus. Now they came

themselves. A lawyer, an expert in the Law, posed the next question.

### The Lawyer's Question (vv. 34–36)

The lawyer asked Jesus what He considered to be the greatest of the Law's commandments.

### Jesus' Answer (vv. 37–40)

This is the first controversy in which Jesus gave a straight answer to a question. Without hesitation, Jesus quoted Deut. 6:5, a verse repeated daily by devout Jews. He went on to quote a related commandment from Lev. 19:18, which commanded that a person should love his neighbor as he loved himself.

Jesus' point was that a person could not love God without also loving his neighbor. Neither could a person really love his neighbor unless he first loved God.

Jesus based His argument on Ps. 110:1, assuming with the Judaism of His time the accuracy of the Davidic superscription and the inspiration of the actual text itself, which would imply its truthfulness. Jewish tradition recognized Ps. 110 as messianic in nature. It referred to the Messiah as a transcendent being who would sit at God's right hand, not as a military leader.

■ *If a person loves God with all his being loves*
■ *his fellowman as he loves himself, he will*
■ *keep all of God's commandments.*

## A QUESTION FOR THE PHARISEES (22:41–46)

Having answered the questions of the Pharisees and Sadducees, it was now Jesus' turn to do the questioning. Facing the gathered Pharisees, He asked their opinion about "the Christ." "Whose son is he?" (v. 41), He asked.

They replied, "The son of David." The Pharisees' answer set up Jesus' real question. That question was: If the Messiah is merely the human offspring of David, why does David himself speak of Him as "Lord"—a master or sovereign above the one who is king of Israel and the highest human authority in the land?

Matthew tells us that no one dared ask Him questions from that time on.

- *The Pharisees' concept of the Messiah was too*
- *limited. They needed to see that the Messiah*
- *could be both transcendent, heavenly Lord as*
- *well as the human descendant of David.*

## QUESTIONS TO GUIDE YOUR STUDY

1. What is the point of the parable of the wedding feast?
2. Jesus answered questions about paying taxes to Caesar. Is His answer applicable to our present-day tax obligations?
3. Why are the "two greatest command-ments" so important to God?

## MATTHEW 23

Chapter 23 begins Jesus' final discourse that takes place in two parts. This chapter is the first part.

### CRITICISM OF THE SCRIBES AND PHARISEES (23:1–12)

Speaking to His disciples and to the gathered crowd, Jesus exposed the faults of some of the scribes and Pharisees.

### A Warning (vv. 2–3)

Jesus told His audience to pay attention to the teachings of these religious leaders. After all, they sat in "Moses' seat," the chair in the synagogue from which the Law's meaning was interpreted. But these leaders did not always practice what they preached.

### Faults of the Leaders (vv. 4–10)

Several other characteristics of the scribes and Pharisees disturbed Jesus. For instance, they loved to show off their piety. They had to have an audience for everything they did.

### What Makes a Person Great (vv. 11–12)

Once again Jesus repeated the principle He had often taught before. The truly great person is one who serves others.

## A SERIES OF ACCUSATIONS (23:13–36)

In the following series of seven accusations, each preceded by "woe to you," Jesus continued to criticize the hypocrisy He saw in the lives of the scribes and Pharisees. These "woes" were expressions of grief and sorrow uttered out of concern for the wrongs these religious leaders were doing to other people and for the punishment they were about to bring on themselves.

### Shutting People Out of the Kingdom (v. 13)

Jesus first accused the leaders of shutting people out of God's kingdom. They refused to accept Jesus' invitation to enter the kingdom by faith and repentance, and they kept others from doing so as well.

**Oaths**

Jesus raised the oath to a new level of understanding. See Matthew 5:33–37. At His trial before Caiaphas, Jesus was silent to the questions until a binding oath was placed upon Him. See Matthew 26:63–65. Jesus did not condemn oaths, only the abuse of God's name in the taking of oaths.

### The Problem of Proselytes (v. 15)

In Jesus' day, Judaism had a missionary dimension. Jesus said the scribes and Pharisees would "travel over land and sea to win a single convert." But then they would weigh down that convert under their Law, making him twice as legalistic as themselves.

### Insincere Oaths (vv. 16–22)

The leaders had, in a sense, made perjury legal with their teachings on oaths. For example, if a person swore by the temple, he did not have to keep his oath. Jesus recognized that no matter what a person might swear by, all belonged to God; therefore, the person who swore was calling God as a witness to his promise and was bound by the oath.

### Tithing the Little; Neglecting the Great (vv. 23–24)

While meticulously tithing these tiny herbs, the scribes had neglected the truly important aspects of the Law such as justice, mercy, and faithfulness (v. 23).

### Only Clean on the Outside (vv. 25–26)

Jesus compared the Jewish leaders to cups and plates that are clean on the outside but dirty on the inside.

### Like Whitewashed Tombs (vv. 27–28)

Jesus saw that the scribes and Pharisees were like those whitewashed tombs. On the outside all appeared to be well. Inside, however, they were full of decay.

Before Passover, tombs were whitewashed not only to beautify them, but so pilgrims could see them easily and not be defiled by walking on them.

### Completing the Work of Their Fathers (vv. 29–36)

Now Jesus' judgment on the leaders reached its zenith. The ancestors of the Jewish leaders had killed the prophets God had sent to them. But they were about to complete their fathers' work by killing Jesus and others who would come in His name.

■ *The seven "woes" (accusations) by Jesus*
■ *were a collective criticism of the hypocrisy of*
■ *Israel's Jewish leaders. His accusations reach*
■ *a climax as He shows a solidarity between*

■ the current Jewish leaders and their prede-
■ cessors who murdered the prophets of God.

## A LAMENT FOR JERUSALEM (23:37–39)

Knowledge of Jerusalem's approaching destruction filled Jesus with the deepest sorrow. Jesus had hoped to take the children of Israel under His wing and nurture them like a mother hen does her baby chicks. But they were not willing, and so would face their judgment.

■ *God never imposes His love by overriding*
■ *human will. Unbelieving Israel had chosen*
■ *its own destiny.*

## QUESTIONS TO GUIDE YOUR STUDY

1. What plagued the scribes and Pharisees to cause them to be so consistently hypocritical?
2. Describe a great person according to verses 11–12. What are some examples of great people?
3. Where do Pharisaical attitudes surface in today's church? What is our best response toward hypocrisy?

# MATTHEW 24

## A PREDICTION AND TWO QUESTIONS (24:1–3)

### Jesus' Prediction (v. 1)

As they left the temple, Jesus' followers marveled at its grandeur (cf. Luke 21:5). Jesus predicted what might have seemed inconceivable at the time—the temple would soon be destroyed.

### The Disciples' Questions (vv. 2–3)

During their conversation, two questions surfaced regarding Jesus' coming and the end of the age.

*Question 1.* When they rested on the hillside, the disciples naturally questioned when such a catastrophe would occur. "Tell us, when will this happen?" (v. 3).

*Question 2.* "What will be the sign of your coming and of the end of the age?" (v. 3).

■ *Jesus will make clear that the destruction of*
■ *the temple and the end of the age are two sep-*
■ *arate events. Because the disciples could*
■ *scarcely imagine that one could occur with-*
■ *out the other, they considered both questions*
■ *one and the same.*

### A WARNING NOT TO MISREAD EVENTS (24:4–14)

Jesus' answer to the disciples' questions first addressed the question about the sign of the end of the age. He warned His disciples not to allow themselves to be led astray by the many false messiahs that would come.

The time between Jesus' earthly life and the earth's end time would be marked also by sufferings in the church. Persecutions and executions of Christians would occur. Partly because of these, many within the church would lose faith and love and be misled by false prophets.

In A.D. 70 during the siege and fall of Jerusalem, the commanding Roman general, Titus, tried to save the temple. He gave orders "to club down anyone who disobeyed his orders, but the soliders, driven by their hatred of the Jews and the hope of finding riches in the temple, were not to be restrained."

Cleon L. Rogers, Jr. in *The Topical Josephus,* (Grand Rapids: Zondervan, 1992), p. 195.

*The period of time before Christ's return will be characterized by a growing polarization between good and evil. God's people will increase in power, witness, and impact in the world, even as persecution and hostility intensify and global conditions deteriorate. The end will come only after the gospel is "preached in the whole world as a testimony to all nations" (v. 14).*

## ABOUT JERUSALEM'S COMING DESTRUCTION (24:15–28)

### *The Destruction of the Temple (vv. 15–20)*

Not yet having answered the Disciples' second question, Jesus next launched into an explanation about the coming destruction of Jerusalem. He spoke of the *desolating sacrilege* as a sign that it was time to flee the city. This event is commonly known as the "Abomination of Desolation." The only advance notice of this event Jesus gave involves an event that will profane the temple, fulfilling the prophecy of Dan. 9:27.

### *Tribulation (vv. 21–28)*

Escape will become all-important, for Jerusalem's destruction will be associated with great tribulation. Destruction will arrive so quickly that believers must waste no time fleeing from the city.

*Jesus predicted the coming destruction of Jerusalem. The very temple itself would be profaned and then destroyed.*

**Herod's Temple**

Herod's temple was the third one built in Jerusalem. Solomon's was first; Zerubbabel's, second. Construction on Herod's temple began around 20 B.C. The main structure was completed within ten years. The decoration and finishing continued until A.D. 64, more than thirty years after Jesus' crucifixion.
William H. Stephens

**Tribulation**

The word *tribulation* refers to a particular time of suffering associated with events of the end time. It will surpass any trouble yet experienced in human history (Matt. 24:21).

# SIGNS OF CHRIST'S SECOND COMING (24:29–31)

Jesus warned His disciples against believing that wars, earthquakes, and famines were signs of the end. But He did tell them the signs that would announce His coming at the end of the age. Jesus portrayed His return in the imagery of cosmic upheaval. The universe will no longer continue as it has. His imagery may well point to overthrow of the cosmic and demonic powers often associated in paganism with the sun, moon, and stars.

## THE FIG TREE'S LESSON (24:32–35)

Jesus used the fig tree as an illustration of a sign pointing to a coming event. He reminded His disciples that the appearance of leaves on a fig tree means "that summer is near" (v. 32). In a similar way, He told them the occurrence of "these things" would mean His coming is near—"right at the door" (v. 33). This is a difficult text to interpret.

## WATCH AND BE READY! (24:36–44)

Jesus told His disciples that the exact hour and day of His second coming were known only to God the Father. Even He, God's Son, did not share the knowledge of the time of the end.

- We do not know when Christ will return. It
- is imperative then that we remain prepared
- for His coming.

Abomination of Desolation

This term dates back to the Old Testament. It refers to that which is detestable to God and is particularly related to idolatry. The English word *abomination* translates four Hebrew and one Greek word. Those words mean "stinking, rotten," "a detested thing," and "offensive, detestable." It is a special term used in the books of Daniel, Matthew, Mark, Luke, and Revelation. In Daniel, the word for "desolation" is *shomem*, which has two root meanings. One meaning is "to be desolated, ravaged," and the second is "to be appalled, astounded." The original passage in Daniel serves as the textual and historical precedent for later applications. The passages in the Gospels and Revelation point ahead to the destruction of Jerusalem in A.D. 69–70.

Jesus' first coming to earth had been in the form of the Suffering Servant. But all the people will see Him in His second coming as the heavenly Son of Man prophesied in Dan. 7:13–14. All will see Him coming on heaven's clouds with glory and power. It will be a magnificent, majestic event. It is natural to understand this coming as described in Rev. 19:11–16. Jesus explained the signs that will mark His return. His second coming will be a majestic event, marked by His glorious appearance and the joining of the redeemed in heaven with His faithful people on the earth.

## A CHALLENGE TO FAITHFULNESS (24:45–51)

Jesus illustrated His point about preparedness with a detailed, three-pronged parable. This parable contrasts a faithful servant with a wicked servant.

- *The faithful servant was rewarded, and the*
- *unfaithful servant was punished. God has*
- *commanded all individuals to be good stew-*
- *ards of His creation, and therefore holds us*
- *all accountable.*

## QUESTIONS TO GUIDE YOUR STUDY

1. What would signal the destruction of the temple?
2. How will Christ's Second Coming differ from His first?
3. What should be the attitude of believers toward Jesus' return?

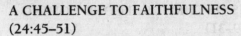

# MATTHEW 25

This chapter presents a collection of three parables.

## THE PARABLE OF THE WISE AND THE FOOLISH MAIDENS (25:1–13)

Jesus used a parable about a wedding to emphasize the need for preparation for His return. The main characters in this parable are ten maidens awaiting the arrival of the bridegroom. All ten carried lamps since the festivities were taking place at night. The imagery of the parable accurately reflects typical customs of first-century Palestinian wedding festivities.

But the bridegroom did not come when expected. Because of the delay, the maidens slept. At midnight, however, they were awakened by the news that the bridegroom was finally coming. Little oil was left in the maidens' lamps after the long wait. This was no problem for five of the maidens who had wisely brought flasks of oil. But the other five had not prepared for a possible delay, and they had no extra oil.

The five who had extra oil had only enough for themselves. They told the others to go and buy more. Although it was midnight, it was possible that all the villagers were out for the wedding celebration and some merchant might have been willing to sell them oil. By the time these five maidens returned from buying oil, the bridegroom had already come. He and his procession had already gone to the marriage feast, and the door was closed. The bridegroom refused to let latecomers come in.

"The Lord himself will come down from heaven with a loud command, with the voice of the archangel, and with the trumpet call of God" (1 Thess. 4:16, NCV).

 Jesus' advice to His followers was to "keep watch" (v. 42). That is, be prepared for His coming, since they could not know the time of His return.

ℕ

- This parable emphasizes that each believer
- has a personal responsibility to remain faithful to God and to prepare for His return.

**Talent**

A measure of weight of money in silver or gold. It was the highest known denomination of currency in the ancient Roman Empire.

## THE PARABLE OF THE TALENTS (25:14–30)

Jesus told another parable to emphasize the importance of responsibly using one's God-given gifts in the time before Christ's return. He spoke of a man who was getting ready for a journey. Before he left, the man turned his assets over to three of his servants for management in his absence. These assets were given in the form of "talents." Today, we call a person's abilities "talents" because of this parable.

This master gave his most capable servant five talents to manage. The second most capable servant received two talents. And the third received one talent. The servant with five talents used his money so well that he doubled it. The servant with two talents did the same. But the servant with one talent, fearful of losing the money, buried it in the ground.

When the master returned after a long absence, he called in the three servants for an accounting. He had praise for the first two servants, who had doubled their talents. They had handled their assets so capably that he rewarded them with even greater responsibility. The third servant tried to excuse his failure to use the master's money productively. His reason for fear of investing had come from his knowledge that the master was "a hard man" (v. 24). The master had nothing but condemnation for this servant. He took that servant's one talent and gave it to the servant who had ten.

Those who make use of what they have will receive even more; those who fail to use what they have will lose what they have.

- Each individual is responsible for the use of
- only those gifts and abilities which God has
- given him or her.

## THE PARABLE OF THE SHEEP AND THE GOATS (25:31–46)

This is the last of Jesus' parables in Matthew's narrative. It is a parable about the final judgment.

The parable pictures Jesus as the heavenly Son of Man, seated on the throne, surrounded by angels. In the parable, Jesus is described as Judge, King, and Shepherd. As the people of all nations stand before Him, Jesus will make a separation. He will act as a shepherd in separating the goats from the sheep. In this parable, sheep symbolize God's righteous people, and goats symbolize the unrighteous.

In the last judgment, Jesus will put the sheep at His right hand, the place of favor. The goats will be at His left. He will invite the sheep to share in His Father's kingdom because of their ministry to Him on earth. He will declare that they had fed Him, quenched His thirst, and welcomed Him when He was a stranger. The righteous will be totally surprised. When, they will ask, had they ever done these things for Jesus? He will tell them that in performing acts of kindness for those in need, they performed them for Him.

For the goats on the left, the verdict is different, although the criteria for judgment is the same. They are to have the "eternal fire" because they did not care for Jesus when He was suffering. These, too, will question Jesus. They will not remember

Sheep and Goats

Sheep. Sheep were the prominent animals in the sacrificial sytem of Israel. They were also a valuable source of food and clothing.

Goats. Goats are extremely destructive to vegetation and contribute to erosion, as they tear plants out of the soil.

Sheep and goats grazed in the same pasture, and freely mingled. From a distance, they often looked similar in appearance. But it was necessary for Palestinian shepherds to separate the herds because male goats were often hostile toward the sheep.

Jesus contrasted sheep and goats. In His parable of the sheep and goats (Matt. 25:31–46), sheep symbolize God's righteous people, and goats symbolize the unrighteous.

seeing Jesus sick, needy, thirsty, or hungry. Jesus will tell them that He was present in all the suffering people they encountered. By not ministering to them, they failed to minister to Him.

 God will one day judge the entire world, based on their response to the gospel.

- *There are two kinds of people in the world*
- *who will be distinguished on the basis of their*
- *response to the gospel and its emissaries.*
- *Proper responses are rewarded; improper*
- *responses lead to eternal punishment.*

## QUESTIONS TO GUIDE YOUR STUDY

1. The parable of the ten maidens holds what lesson for us?
2. The parable of the talents is well known. What important lessons emerge from this parable?
3. Contrast sheep and goats. What is the main point of the parable of the sheep and goats?

**Passover**

The first of three annual Hebrew festivals. It commemorated the final plague on Egypt when the firstborn of the Egyptians died and the Israelites were spared because of the blood smeared on the doorposts (Exod. 12).

# MATTHEW 26

This chapter begins Matthew's final block of narrative. The key elements in this part of the narrative are the Passion and Crucifixion (26:1–27:66), and Jesus' resurrection (28:1–20).

## A PREDICTION AND A PLOT (26:1–5)

### *The Prediction (vv. 1–2)*

At the end of Jesus' teaching on the Mount of Olives, He predicted for the fourth time (according to Matthew's record) that He would soon die. This time He added something new to His prediction. His death by crucifixion would take place during Passover, only two days away.

### The Plot (vv. 3–5)

Meanwhile, the elders and chief priests, members of the Sanhedrin (the Jewish high court), were plotting Jesus' death. They met at the palace of Caiaphas, who was then high priest. These religious leaders were agreed on the necessity of putting Jesus to death, but the timing was a problem for them.

■ *Feeling more and more threatened by Jesus,*
■ *the religious leaders took bolder steps. They*
■ *decided to meet so they could plot Jesus'*
■ *death.*

## AN ANOINTING AT BETHANY (26:6–13)

At Bethany, Jesus was at the home of a man called Simon the leper. No doubt Simon was a former leper, cured perhaps by Jesus. During the meal at Simon's house, a woman took an alabaster flask of perfume (likely her most valuable possession) and poured it on Jesus' head. From John's account, we know this woman was Mary of Bethany.

**Bethany**

Located on the Mount of Olives' eastern slope, Bethany was about two miles southeast of Jersualem. Bethany was the last stop before Jerusalem just off the main east-west road coming from Jericho.

■ *Mary's loving, generous act was a ministry to*
■ *Jesus. It possibly was her last opportunity to*
■ *minister to Jesus before His death. Her atti-*
■ *tude was in contrast to the critical attitude of*
■ *the disciples.*

99

## JUDAS'S OFFER OF BETRAYAL (26:14–16)

The religious authorities had been looking for an opportunity to arrest Jesus without creating a disturbance among the people. Their objective became unexpectedly easier when Judas came to the chief priests with an offer to betray Jesus. The chief priests agreed to pay Judas thirty shekels, the price of a slave. Matthew writes that from that time on, Judas looked for a chance to betray Jesus.

■ *For a bribe offer of thirty skekels, the price of*
■ *a slave, Judas agreed to betray Jesus and turn*
■ *Him over to the religious authorities.*

## PREPARATIONS FOR THE PASSOVER MEAL (26:17–19)

**Passover Meal**

The lamb for the meal (if this was a complete Passover dinner) had to be slaughtered that afternoon at the temple. The meal would begin at six o'clock that evening.

The disciples asked Jesus for instructions about preparing the Passover meal. This meal had to be eaten within the city of Jerusalem. Because space was at a premium, guests who had traveled to the city for the feast had to borrow rooms from residents.

■ *The disciples plan a Passover meal, which*
■ *will be Jesus' and the disciples' final hours*
■ *together. This "Last Supper" takes place in a*
■ *large upper room of a house.*

## A FORETELLING OF BETRAYAL (26:20–25)

That night Jesus and His disciples shared the Passover meal. As they ate, Jesus solemnly told

His disciples that one of them would betray Him. Judas had kept his plans secret from the other disciples, but Jesus knew his heart. This news greatly upset the disciples. Except for Judas, each asked Jesus, "Surely not I, Lord?" (v. 22).

Although Jesus did not identify His betrayer, He did say that one who had dipped food into the dish with Him would betray Him. No doubt several of them had already done so by this time.

It was at this point that Judas asked, "Teacher, I'm not the one, am I?" Jesus replied, "You have said it yourself" (v. 25, NLT).

Jesus went on to say that He would fulfill the role of which the prophets had written. He would be the Suffering Servant and Shepherd dying for His sheep (see Isa. 53:3–8 and Zech. 13:7). Although He was fulfilling His role, He lamented the fate of His betrayer. He was possibly giving Judas one last chance to repent.

■ *Judas is revealed as the one who will betray*
■ *Jesus to the religious authorities. With full*
■ *knowledge that Jesus is aware of what is about*
■ *to happen, Judas proceeds with his plan.*

## THE BREAD AND THE CUP (26:26–29)

After sundown on Thursday, Jesus and His disciples relaxed to enjoy the Passover meal. During the meal, Jesus took, blessed, and broke bread. As He gave it to His disciples, He told them to eat the bread. It represented His body. Soon that body would be given for them in death. After the disciples said a prayer of thanksgiving, He gave the cup to His disciples, telling them all to drink from it. The cup represented Jesus' "blood of the covenant" (v. 28), which would soon be "poured out for many for the forgiveness of sins."

Jesus saw this meal as a foretaste of the meal He would someday share with His followers in the kingdom of His Father.

**The Lord's Supper**

The terms *eucharist*, *thanksgiving*, or *communion* are often applied to the Lord's Supper, and each highlights a specific aspect of this ordinance. "The Lord's Supper" appears more satisfactory for the overall designation, reminding Christians that they share the loaf and cup at His table, not their own.

Paul emphasized the memorial aspect of the supper: "Do this in remembrance of me." Christians were to remember that the body of Christ was broken (bread) and His blood shed (cup) for them. As the Passover was a symbol of the old covenant, the Lord's Supper is a symbol of the new. Christians remember the sacrifice provided for their deliverance from bondage and look forward to the ultimate consummation in the land of promise, the kingdom of God.

This last meal, meanwhile, was a pledge of the certainty of the kingdom's establishment and their sharing together in it.

■ *The celebration of the Lord's Supper signaled*
■ *two important points, one of which looks*
■ *backward while the other is forward-looking.*
■ *(1) As we look back, we commemorate Jesus'*
■ *redemptive death; (2) as we look ahead, we*
■ *anticipate His return with all the redeemed.*

## A PREDICTION OF DENIAL (26:30–35)

After Jesus and the disciples finished the Passover meal, they sang a hymn, probably taken from Psalms 115–118, which formed part of the Passover liturgy.

Jesus then prophesied that the disciples would be scattered. Peter confirmed his loyalty to Jesus, protesting that he would never fall away. But Jesus knew better. Jesus told him that during the night, before the rooster crowed in the morning, Peter would deny Him three times. The others voiced their loyalty as well. John's Gospel tells us that Judas had left the group during the Passover meal.

■ *Peter would have likely fought and died for*
■ *Jesus that night if Jesus had declared Himself*
■ *a military Messiah and ordered a revolt*
■ *against Rome. But Peter would find himself*
■ *unequal to testing when it came in an unex-*
■ *pected form.*

# A TIME OF AGONIZING PRAYER
# (26:36–46)

## *The Scene at Gethsemane (vv. 36–38)*

Jesus went with His disciples to Gethsemane, probably a garden on the Mount of Olives. Jesus wanted to pray and instructed His disciples to stay outside, but He took His three closest disciples—Peter, James, and John—with Him.

## *Jesus' Prayers and the Disciples' Weakness (vv. 39–44)*

Walking a short distance from the three, Jesus fell prostrate to the ground. His prayer, in summary, asked His Father if there were any other way to accomplish the mission He was sent to accomplish. Certainly on His mind was the gruesome method of execution awaiting Him. His greater agony was the anticipation of bearing the world's sins.

## *The Meaning of This Time of Prayer (vv. 45–46)*

No other recorded experience of Jesus reveals His human side so vividly. It is only because He endured such human agony and testing that He can strengthen us in our times of sorrow and temptation and sympathize with us.

Many of Matthew's underlying themes converge here at the garden. God is in control of all these events, however tragic they may seem to others. Jesus is the Son of God who is suffering and dying. His death is humiliating but voluntary, an act of obedience fulfilling God's will.

"In the days of His flesh, He offered up both prayers and supplications with loud crying and tears to the One able to save Him from death, and He was heard because of His piety." (Heb. 5:7, NASB).

Jesus told them about the anguish He was experiencing. He was overwhelmed with sorrow and described it as being as great as death's sorrow. Luke 22:44 describes the extent of His suffering as "to the point of death." Jesus wanted these disciples' human sympathy and support to help Him through His ordeal, so He asked them to watch with Him.

103

## ARREST IN THE GARDEN (26:47–56)

Judas arrived at the garden with an armed crowd ready to arrest Jesus. The crowd evidently consisted of the temple guard and servants of the high priest. Because those who came to make the arrest did not know Jesus, Judas had agreed to identify Jesus with a sign. He would kiss Jesus, as was customary for a disciple greeting his master.

"He willingly gave his life and was treated like a criminal. But he carried away the sins of many people and asked forgiveness for those who sinned." (Isa. 53:12b NCV).

Even in the face of Judas's treachery, Jesus reacted with sadness instead of anger. He called Judas "friend," still holding open the door of repentance. However, Jesus had no intention of resisting arrest. He saw it as fulfilling Isa. 53:12.

Confronted with Jesus' failure to resist and His refusal to let them fight for Him, all the disciples fled. Jesus would have to face His ordeal alone.

■ *Jesus' obvious submission to His arrest*
■ *emphasizes His sovereignty and the volun-*
■ *tary submission to His death.*

## AT CAIAPHAS'S PALACE (26:57–68)

Caiaphas

Son-in-law of Annas, who was High Priest from A.D. 6–15. Caiaphas was appointed around A.D. 18 and removed about A.D. 36.

Matthew now describes the illegal hearing Jesus received at the palace of the high priest, Caiaphas. Peter, having fled with the rest of the disciples, now returned to see what was happening. He remained in the high priest's courtyard.

The high priest put Jesus under oath and demanded that Jesus tell the council whether He was "the Christ, the Son of God" (v. 63).

Jesus' response was, "It is as you say" (v. 64). To the high priest, these were words of blasphemy.

He tore his clothes as an indication that he was hearing blasphemy. Jesus had equated Himself with God.

Those present then blindfolded Jesus and followed with a round of abuse. They spat in His face (a serious insult) and Hit him, and said, "Prophesy to us, Christ. Who hit you" (v. 68). In this experience, Matthew explains that Jesus fulfilled the prophecy of Isa. 50:6.

"I gave my back to those who strike Me, and My cheeks to those who pluck out the beard. I did not cover My face from humiliation and spitting" (Isa. 50:6 NASB).

■ *The illegal council meeting had accom-*
■ *plished its purpose. The Jewish leaders now*
■ *had their "charge" against Jesus. They could*
■ *now take the trial to the next level.*

## PETER'S DENIAL (26:69–75)

Jesus was being tried inside the high priest's palace, but outside, Peter was going through a painful trial of his own. As Peter sat in the high priest's courtyard, a servant girl approached him. She remarked that Peter had been with Jesus. Peter denied her statement to all in the courtyard. He then remained in the courtyard.

Later, another servant girl told bystanders that Peter had been with Jesus. This time Peter swore an oath that he did not even know Jesus.

Still later, a bystander accused Peter of being a follower of Jesus. With even greater intensity, Peter swore that he did not know Jesus. Immediately a rooster crowed. Peter remembered Jesus' prediction of denial. Overwhelmed at his disloyalty, he "wept bitterly" (v. 75).

■ *While Jesus holds up under life-threatening*
■ *conditions, Peter fails miserably under less*
■ *threatening conditions.*

## QUESTIONS TO GUIDE YOUR STUDY

1. Why was there controversy about Mary's anointing of Jesus? What was Jesus' attitude about it?
2. Why was the Gethsemane experience so agonizing for Jesus? What made this time necessary?
3. What are the signs that Jesus voluntarily submitted to the events which led to His death?

**Sanhedrin**

The highest Jewish council in the first century. The council had 71 members and was presided over by the high priest. Both Sadducees and Pharisees were members of this council.

At this time, the Sanhedrin lacked the power to put a person to death (see John 18:31). But Rome would never execute a person on a charge of blasphemy, because that charge pertained only to Jewish Law.

## MATTHEW 27 . . . . . . . . . . . . . . . .

### JESUS' SENTENCING BY THE JEWS (27:1–2)

Early the next morning, the Sanhedrin met again, this time officially and legally. The meeting seems to have been for the purpose of deciding what charge to bring against Jesus so the Romans would put Him to death.

At this point, Matthew interjects a section about Judas's death before continuing his account of Jesus' appearance coming before Pontius Pilate, the Roman governor.

■ *The religious leaders officially meet to decide*
■ *what charges to bring against Jesus. The San-*

■ hedrin decides to bring Jesus before Pontius
■ Pilate, the Roman governor of the region.

## JUDAS'S TRAGIC END (27:3–10)

Realizing that Jesus had been condemned, Judas repented of his act of betrayal. He returned the thirty silver shekels to the elders and chief priests. He confessed to them that Jesus was innocent, and that in betraying Him, he had sinned.

When Judas realized that the religious authorities were not going to reconsider their actions against Jesus, in anger and despair he threw the money down in the temple and left. Seeing no relief for his guilt, Judas committed suicide by hanging himself.

The chief priests collected the coins, but refused to keep the money because they considered it "blood money" and unclean. They finally agreed to use the money to buy a field for the burial of strangers who might die while in Jerusalem. Matthew saw this as fulfilling Old Testament Scripture. (See Jer. 32:7–8 and Zech. 11:12–13.)

■ *Judas repented to the chief priest his*
■ *betrayal of Jesus, admitting that Jesus was*
■ *an innocent man. Filled with guilt, Judas*
■ *hanged himself. Refusing to ask forgiveness*
■ *from God, his guilt became more than he*
■ *could bear.*

## JESUS BEFORE PILATE (27:11–26)

Matthew now resumes the narrative where he left off in verse 2. Pilate, the Roman governor of Judea, was in Jerusalem at the time, although his official residence was in Caesarea. So the religious leaders delivered Jesus to him.

### Questions from Pilate (vv. 11–14)

Pilate's first question: "Are you the king of the Jews?" (v. 11). Pilate's only concern was whether Jesus had broken Roman law.

Jesus' silence fulfilled the prophecy in Isa. 53:7, which says in speaking of the Suffering Servant, "He was oppressed and treated harshly, yet He never said a word" (NLT).

**The Phases of Jesus' Illegal Trial**

1. The religious leaders had already passed a death sentence for Jesus before the trial began (John 11:50; Mark 14:1).
2. The leaders used false witnesses to testify against Jesus (Matt. 26:59).
3. No defense for Jesus was allowed (Luke 22:67–71).
4. The trial took place at night, a violation of Jewish laws (Mark 14:53–65; 15:1).
5. The high priest put Jesus under oath, but then incriminated Him for what He said (Matt. 26:63–66).
6. Serious charges were to be tried only in the high council's regular meeting place, not in the high priest's palace (Mark 14:53–65).

Jesus answered, "Yes, it is as you say" (v. 11). After His answer, the religious authorities hurled their accusations at Jesus. But He refused to reply to their charges.

Pilate's second question: "Don't you hear the testimony they are bringing against you?" Jesus remained silent, which surprised Pilate.

### Jesus or Barabbas (vv. 15–23)

Evidently, Pilate remained unimpressed with the case against Jesus. He saw no evidence of treason. At Passover, it was customary for the governor to release a prisoner for the people. Pilate took advantage of this custom to try to win the crowd's approval for Jesus' release. A man named Barabbas was in prison on charges of murder and insurrection. Pilate offered the crowd a choice to release either Jesus or Barabbas.

During this proceeding, a message reached Pilate from his wife. She had a dream about Jesus that greatly disturbed her. She warned her husband not to prosecute this innocent man.

### Pilate's Decision (vv. 24–26)

Pilate found himself in a quandary. He had a potentially serious riot on his hands if he went ahead and released Jesus. He needed to keep the peace in Jerusalem if he wanted to retain his position as governor. And he needed the support of the religious leaders who were urging Jesus' crucifixion. Yet Pilate must have realized the sentencing of an innocent man to death was a betrayal of Roman justice.

Pilate, however, was too insecure to uphold principles of Roman law or follow his wife's intuition. When Pilate asked the crowd what he should do with Jesus, the people cried out for His death by crucifixion: "Crucify him!"

Pilate literally "washed his hands" of the matter, using this Jewish custom to proclaim his innocence.

- Pilate let the crowd make the choice: Jesus or
- Barabbas? They chose to free a murderer
- rather than the One who came to save them
- from sin. Jesus would be executed for the
- crime for which Barabbas was guilty.

## MOCKING BY ROMAN SOLDIERS (27:27–31)

At this point, Pilate's soldiers took Jesus into the governor's palace, where He faced more mocking and ridicule. They were then ready to take Jesus to the site of His crucifixion.

## THE EXECUTION OF JESUS AT GOLGOTHA (27:32–44)

A convicted criminal was expected to carry the horizontal beam for his own cross to the site of the crucifixion, where the vertical beam was already in the ground. Apparently, Jesus was too weak and injured from His flogging to carry it very far. The soldiers had Simon of Cyrene help carry the crossbeam.

The crucifixion took place at Golgotha, meaning "the place of the skull." There, Jesus' hands and feet were nailed to the cross between two robbers, who may have been followers of Barabbas. Over Jesus' head was placed a wooden placard reading, "THIS IS JESUS, THE KING OF THE JEWS" (v. 37). While He hung on the cross, Jesus was offered a pain-killing drink, but He

The soldiers followed the usual custom of casting lots (perhaps variously marked pebbles) for Jesus' clothes. This fulfilled the words of Ps. 22:18, "They divide my garments among them and cast lots for my clothing."

Death by Crucifixion

The method the Romans used to execute Christ was the most painful and degrading form of capital punishment in the ancient world. A person crucified in Jesus' day was first beaten with a whip consisting of thongs with embedded pieces of metal. This scourging was designed to hasten death and lessen the terrible ordeal. After the beating, the victim carried the crossbeam to signify that life was over and to break his will to live. A tablet detailing the crime was often placed around the criminal's neck. At the site, the prisoner was tied (normal method) or nailed (if a quicker death was desired) to the crossbeam.

refused it, allowing Him to maintain a clear and fully conscious mind.

While on the cross, in the midst of His greatest physical agony, Jesus faced ridicule from three different groups: passersby, religious leaders, and the two robbers beside Him. One of the taunts from the crowd was, "If you are the Son of God" (v. 40)—an exact reproduction of Satan's catcall in Matt. 4:3, during Jesus' temptations in the wilderness.

- Jesus endured extreme pain and ridicule from
- the soldiers, the religious leaders, and the
- crowd. He willingly submitted to this abuse
- as part of His mission.

## THE DEATH OF JESUS (27:45–50)

At Jesus' death, three unusual events took place: unnatural darkness, the rending of the temple veil, and the resurrection of the saints.

### Darkness (vv. 45–46)

From noon until three o'clock in the afternoon, the land was covered in darkness. This is the first of three remarkable events in nature associated with His death and reflecting its cosmic significance. Perhaps this darkness was symbolic of God's judgment upon those who had rejected His Son. It isn't surprising that nature reacted with darkness during the hours when the Creator hung dying on the cross.

### Jesus Gives Up His Spirit (vv. 47–50)

At about three o'clock, Jesus cried out the words of Ps. 22:1: "My God, my God, why have you forsaken me?" This cry of Jesus is the only one of Jesus'

sayings from the cross preserved by Matthew and Mark. Others are recorded by Luke's and John's Gospels. God the Father was there in this entire event, using it to reconcile the world to Himself. But Jesus was bearing the sin of the world. The One who had been totally free from sin was now bearing the world's sin.

Then, after a loud cry, Jesus yielded His spirit. Luke records, "Father, into your hands I commit my spirit" (23:46). John records, "It is finished" (19:30).

## ACCOMPANYING EVENTS (27:51–56)

### *Rending of the Temple Veil (v. 51)*
The veil at the entrance to the Holy of Holies was split "from top to bottom" (v. 51). This rending of the temple curtain can symbolize the opening of direct access to God because of Jesus' death.

Temple Veil

This curtain separated the Most Holy Place from the Holy Place (2 Chron. 3:14). Only the high priest was able to pass through the veil and then only on the Day of Atonement (Lev. 16:2).

### *Tombs Opened by an Earthquake (vv. 52–53)*
An earthquake split rocks and caused tombs to open. Matthew wrote that after Jesus had been raised from the dead, the bodies of many of God's people buried near Jerusalem were raised.

### *Witnesses to the Events (vv. 54–56)*
Matthew listed followers who witnessed the events of the cross. These included Mary Magdalene and Mary, the mother of James and John. Matthew apparently believed these women deserved credit for their faithfulness by their presence during Jesus' greatest trial and suffering.

■ *Events within the world of nature testified to the*
■ *monumental significance of the Crucifixion.*

111

## BURIAL IN JOSEPH OF ARIMATHEA'S TOMB (27:57–61)

The Jewish Law required that the body of an executed person be buried the same day death occurred. Jesus died about three o'clock on Friday afternoon. It was necessary that He be buried before the Sabbath began at sunset.

Joseph of Arimathea, called a "rich man" by Matthew (v. 57), asked and received permission from Pilate to take the body of Jesus for burial. At least two of Jesus' women followers from Galilee watched as Joseph laid Jesus' body in the tomb and sealed it. These were two of the women, Mary Magdalene and the "other Mary" (v. 61), who had seen the Crucifixion from a distance. (See John 19:39–40 for additional details about Jesus' burial.)

- Jesus' body is finally laid to rest in a stone
- tomb. His burial is witnessed by others, and
- the tomb is sealed.

## THE GUARD (27:62–66)

Only Matthew has left a record of an action taken by the Jewish authorities after Jesus' death.

On the Sabbath, the day after Jesus died, the Pharisees and chief priests went to Pilate with a request. They told Pilate that Jesus had promised to rise from the dead three days after His death. So they feared Jesus' disciples would steal His body and then claim that He had risen. That fraud, they declared, would be even worse than Jesus' fraudulent claim to be the Messiah.

They asked that Pilate make the tomb secure until Jesus had been dead three days. Pilate

"And if a man has committed a sin worthy of death, and he is put to death, and you hang him on a tree, his corpse shall not hang all night on the tree, but you shall surely bury him on the same (for he who is hanged is accused of God), so that you do not defile your land which the Lord your God gives you as an inheritance" (Deut. 21:22–23, NASB).

The Jews believed that death was irrevocable after a person had been dead three days, since by then the spirit had left the body.

agreed to the religious leaders' request. He gave them a group of soldiers to guard the tomb, and the stone at the tomb's entrance was sealed.

■ *The religious authorities took special measures*
■ *to guard against a "fraudulent resurrection" of*
■ *Jesus. In the end, their actions only served to*
■ *add evidence to the event of Jesus' resurrection.*

## QUESTIONS TO GUIDE YOUR STUDY

1. What are your impressions of Jesus' trial? Why didn't Jesus defend Himself?
2. What Old Testament prophecies did Jesus' trial and death fulfill?
3. What was the significance of the natural events that took place at the time of Jesus' death.

## MATTHEW 28

### RESURRECTION! (28:1–7)

Early on Sunday morning, Mary Magdelene and Mary the mother of James and Joseph went back to Jesus' tomb.

The women were greeted by something very different from what they had expected. Either just before or at the time of their arrival at the tomb, "there was a violent earthquake" (v. 2). An angel appeared, rolled the stone away from the entrance and, in triumph, sat on the stone.

According to Mark's and Luke's Gospels, they were bringing spices to anoint Jesus's body (see Mark 16:1; Luke 24:1).

■ *As He had predicted He would, Jesus rose*
■ *from the grave on the third day after His*
■ *death. Jesus had conquered death!*

113

**The Resurrected Body**

Those raised from death have a bodily existence. The earthly body of lowliness will be renewed like the glorious body of the resurrected Jesus, becoming a heavenly body. Resurrection does not mean that the personality dissolves into a larger whole. Rather, it means the total transformation of "flesh and blood" into a "spiritual body," that is, a personality created and formed anew by God's Spirit. The resurrection body is new and unimaginably superior to the earthy body, while it maintains some continuity with life as lived before death and resurrection.

## A MEETING WITH JESUS (28:8–10)

The women quickly left the tomb to carry out the angel's instructions. Fear mingled with the joy they felt as they ran to tell the eleven remaining disciples the news of the Resurrection.

As they went, Jesus Himself met them. This meeting was not merely a vision. The women were able to grasp His feet in an act of worship. He was the Jesus they remembered. But now they recognized Him as deserving worship belonging to God alone.

Jesus repeated the instructions the angel had given the women (v. 7). There was an important change, however. He called His disciples "my brothers" (v. 10). They had failed Him completely in His time of greatest trial. But Jesus forgave them and looked ahead to what they would be as they served Him in the future.

■ *Jesus had risen from the grave! The response*
■ *of the women is worship.*

## A COVER-UP OF THE TRUTH (28:11–15)

Some of the Roman soldiers told the chief priests about the supernatural events that had occurred.

The chief priests decided their best course of action was to bribe the soldiers to cover up the truth. The soldiers accepted the payment and agreed to say they had fallen asleep while on guard, and Jesus' disciples had stolen the body.

Of the four Gospels, only Matthew tells us how the religious authorities answered the fact of the empty tomb. No one denied that the tomb was empty and that Jesus' body could not be found. Matthew declared that even when he was writ-

ing his Gospel, this falsehood was still being cir-
culated to explain Jesus' resurrection.

- *The chief priests learned the truth about the*
- *supernatural events surrounding Jesus' Res-*
- *urrection. They resorted to bribery to fabri-*
- *cate a lie to explain what happened.*

## A WORLDWIDE MISSION (28:16–20)

### *Jesus' Great Commission (vv. 18–19)*

Jesus' commission to His disciples is sand-
wiched between a truth and a promise—which
taken together more than equip disciples for
carrying out the commission.

The truth is that (v. 28) all authority in both
heaven and earth have been given to Jesus. The
promise (v. 30) is that this One who has all
authority is with His disciples—not only now
but until the end of the age.

Disciple

In the Greek world, the
word *disciple* normally
referred to an adherent
of a particular teacher
or religious-
philosophical school. It
was the task of the
disciple to learn, study,
and pass along the
sayings and teachings
of the master.

- *The Great Commission, like the rest of Mat-*
- *thew, defines evangelism as making disciples*
- *who are baptized and who obey all of the*
- *commandments of Jesus.*

## QUESTIONS TO GUIDE YOUR STUDY

1. What evidence does Matthew present
   that Jesus has risen from the grave?
2. What is to be the main activity of the
   Great Commission?
3. What implications does Jesus' promise, "I
   am with you," have for us as we carry out
   His Great Commission?

# REFERENCE SOURCES USED

The following list is a collection of the source works used for this volume. All are from Broadman & Holman's list of published reference resources. They should meet the reader's need for more specific information or for expanded treatment of the Gospel of Matthew.

Blair, Joe. *Introducing the New Testament*, pp. 55–67. A high-level overview of Matthew's Gospel that contains outlines of books, special graphics, maps and photos, and summary questions.

Blomberg, Craig. *Matthew* (The New American Commentary), vol. 22. A more scholarly treatment of the text of Matthew that provides emphases on the text itself, background, and theological considerations.

Crissey, Clair M. *Matthew* (Layman's Bible Book Commentary). A popular-level treatment of Matthew's Gospel. This easy-to-use volume provides a relevant and practical perspective.

*Holman Bible Dictionary*. An exhaustive, alphabetically arranged resource of Bible-related subjects. An excellent tool of definitions and other information on the people, places, things, and events of the Bible.

*Holman Bible Handbook*, pp. 541–67. A comprehensive treatment of Matthew that offers outlines, commentary on key themes and sections, and full-color photos, illustrations, charts, and maps. Provides an emphasis on the broader theological teachings of Matthew.

*Holman Book of Biblical Charts, Maps, and Reconstructions*, pp. 86–87, 95–97. A colorful, visual collection of charts, maps, and reconstructions, these well-designed tools are invaluable to the study of the Bible.

Lea, Thomas D. *The New Testament: Its Background and Message*, pp. 167–280. An excellent resource for background material—political, cultural, historical, and religious. Provides background information in broad strokes on specific books, including the Gospels.

Robertson, A. T. *Word Pictures in the New Testament.* Vol. 1, "Matthew and Mark," pp. 3–246. Insights into the Greek language of the New Testament. Provides word studies as well as grammatical and background insights into Matthew's text.

Robertson, A. T. *A Grammar of the Greek New Testament in the Light of Historical Research.* An exhaustive scholarly work on the underlying language of the New Testament. Provides advanced insights into the grammatical, syntactical, and lexical aspects of the New Testament.